THE POWER OF
STRATEGIC
COSTING

THE POWER OF STRATEGIC COSTING

A Proactive Competitive Approach for Setting Future Strategic Plans

DALE M. BRETHAUER

AMACOM
American Management Association
New York • Atlanta • Boston • Chicago • Kansas City • San Francisco • Washington, D.C.
Brussels • Mexico City • Tokyo • Toronto

Special discounts on bulk quantities of AMACOM books are available to
corporations, professional associations, and other organizations. For details,
contact Special Sales Department, AMACOM, an imprint of AMA
Publications, a division of
American Management Association,
1601 Broadway, New York, NY 10019.
Tel: 212-903-8316   Fax: 212-903-8083

This publication is designed to provide accurate and authoritative information
in regard to the subject matter covered. It is sold with the understanding that the
publisher is not engaged in rendering legal, accounting, or other professional
service. If legal advice or other expert assistance is required, the services
of a competent professional person should be sought.

Brethauer, Dale.
    The power of strategic costing : a proactive competitive approach
    for setting future strategic plans / Dale Brethauer.
        p.   cm.
    Includes bibliographical references and index.
    ISBN 0-8144-0486-3
    1. Cost accounting.   2. Managerial accounting.   I. Title.
    HF5686.C8B67355   99-30854
    65'.42—dc21   CIP

10 9 8 7 6 5 4 3 2 1

CONTENTS

INTRODUCTION

Have you ever put together a jigsaw puzzle? When I begin working on a puzzle, I pour all the pieces out on the table and turn them over so that I can see the part of the picture that each piece represents. Next I get all the outline pieces and put them together so that I have the shape and size of the puzzle. Then I begin filling in the picture.

What does putting a puzzle together have to do with strategic costing? Well, before you actually begin the first step of strategic costing, you need to gather information, become completely familiar with the product or service that you are analyzing, and make sure you have all the data necessary to complete the analysis. (You're turning all the pieces over so you can see the parts of the picture they represent.)

This book contains information that is simple in essence yet broad in application. The costing method presented here is applicable to any size company, from a "Mom & Pop" to a multibillion dollar corporate giant. My objective in writing this book is for you to master the concepts and realize the impact that the Strategic Costing Process can have on the profitability and long-term viability of your business. When you achieve a clear understanding of each step of the process, you will have in your grasp a tool that can ultimately set your company apart from the rest.

The Strategic Costing Process has four steps, which will be covered in extensive detail in the book:

1. Estimate your suppliers' product or service costs.
2. Estimate your competitors' product or service costs.
3. Set your company's target cost sheet and identify areas for process and product improvement.
4. Determine the value to your company of making these process and product changes and continuously improving.

The concepts of the Strategic Costing Process are presented in a simple "how to" manner. Chapter 1 introduces the concepts of strategic costing and develops the reasoning behind it. It begins by identifying the major categories of expenses incurred in producing a product or service then covers two case studies to illustrate the material. Also included is a brief overview of each of the steps in the Strategic Costing Process.

Chapter 2 describes the elements of cost: materials used, direct costs, plant overheads, and general and administrative costs. The elements of cost are similar for both manufacturing and service industries. However, materials are usually the main cost drivers in the manufacturing sector while labor is the main cost driver in service industries.

Chapter 3 describes how to estimate each of the elements of cost using equations based on common industrial factors. (Examples of each calculation are included.) This chapter actually begins the first step of the Strategic Costing Process. (In fact, Chapters 4, 5, and 6 also address the first step.) In order to make the calculations, you must know three things: raw materials needed, number of people required to produce the product or service, and total capital investment. This cost-estimating model has proved exceptionally accurate. A spreadsheet that automatically calculates an estimate of costs is included on the computer disk that comes with this book.

Chapter 4 describes how to gather actual supplier cost data by asking certain questions while touring a supplier's plant. This chapter lists those pertinent questions and takes you on a verbal walk-through of a fictitious plant that produces powder metal bushings. An estimate of the bushing item cost of the supplier is then calculated.

Chapter 5 focuses on using the power and knowledge provided by the estimate of supplier costs to negotiate competitive material pricing. You will learn how to use this power and will be shown how to prepare for a negotiation that achieves a win-win solution.

Chapter 6 includes three case studies using the methods described in the previous chapter. These case studies estimate costs for pepperoni pizza, wooden pallets, and the dry cleaning of a man's shirt. The purpose of Chapter 6 is to illustrate the power of a simple but accurate cost model, which can be used to estimate costs for a myriad of products and services.

Chapter 7 moves on to step 2 of the Strategic Costing Process. It describes how to make a competitive assessment and how to gather the data necessary to calculate competitor costs. Competitive assessment means a thorough study of a competitor's business beyond production costs, including investments, cash flow, financial position, and projected strengths and weaknesses. This information is crucial for setting business strategies, and you will learn how and where to find it. Spreadsheets to assist in calculating cash flow and financial ratios are included on the supplied computer disk.

Chapter 8 describes how to establish a target cost and outlines step 3 of the Strategic Costing Process. You will learn how to calculate competitor costs using the data gathered in chapter 7, compare them with your own company costs, and understand the differences. The target cost sheet, provided in this chapter, is used for this purpose and will help you identify your company's cost areas that need improvement. This information guides you to achieve and maintain a competitive edge.

Chapter 9 discusses the value to the company of implementing a strategic program. The chapter looks at short-term effects and calculates the long-range consequences of business decisions.

Chapter 10 puts it all together using a case study that requires you to set business strategies for a fictitious company and product based on information gained by following the Strategic Costing Process. You are led step by step through the process.

Chapter 11 summarizes all information and methods described in the book and reviews the benefits of using the Strategic Costing Process. It also answers commonly asked questions.

In the following chapters, you'll be uncovering pieces of data, putting together the outline of the picture, and filling in the numbers. Let's get started on the puzzle!

BACKGROUND

1

THE STRATEGIC
COSTING PROCESS

When companies are able to assess their suppliers' product or service costs, they gain powerful insight and control of the purchasing process. Then they are able to take the next step: negotiating lower purchase prices to minimize material costs. Material and labor costs are the biggest components of unit or product total direct costs.[1] So reducing material costs has a major impact on lowering total costs and increasing corporate profits.

After estimating competitors' costs, companies can compare them with their own costs to determine cost areas where they have an advantage or disadvantage with respect to the competition. Determining the variances between a competitor's and your company's product or service costs allows you to use target costs to establish cost goals.[2]

The Strategic Costing Process has four steps:

1. Estimate your suppliers' product or service costs.
2. Estimate your competitors' product or service costs.
3. Set your company's target cost sheet and identify areas for product and process improvement.

---

1. *Direct costs* are costs directly associated with the production of the product or service.
2. *Variances* are the differences between a competitor's estimated costs and your company's costs based primarily on differences in prices per unit or quantity consumed.

3

4. Determine the value to your company of making these process and product changes and continuously improving.

Using the four steps of the process affects the corporate bottom line substantially, guides corporate planning, and helps to set business strategies. It also helps to answer such questions as:

- Should my company expand product capacity?
- How can a supplier alliance affect my company's competitiveness?
- What are my competitors' strengths and weaknesses?
- What strategies will allow my company to be proactive against the competition?
- How will this process affect my company's bottom line and cash flow?
- Should my company be aggressive against the competition or invest in more R&D and improve the process first?
- Should my company be a player in this market?

If you look in any dictionary you find that the term *strategic costing* is not there. If you look at the words separately, however, you discover the core meaning of this phrase:

STRATEGIC:	COST:
1) Of, relating to, or marked by strategy	1) To require expenditure or payment
2) Necessary to or important in the initiation, conduct, or completion of a strategic plan	2) To have a price of
3) Of great importance within an integrated whole or to a planned effect	3) The amount or equivalent paid or charged for something

With these definitions in mind, the following statements can be made about the Strategic Costing Process:

- Strategic costing targets the maximum manufacturing cost that will allow an expected return while enabling a company to gain share within a market niche.
- Using strategic costing, a product manufacturing cost goal can be set that can be used for both strategic analysis and operational control.
- Strategic cost = target price – target profit.
- Strategic costing establishes a cost goal that allows up-front planning with strategic significance.
- Strategic costing identifies ways to reduce overall product cost.

Aggressive companies use the Strategic Costing Process to evaluate and direct efforts to be competitive, improve continuously, and reach optimal performance. A strategic costing system aids in planning future goals, controlling costs and investments, and measuring corporate performance.

The process presented in this book encompasses all the elements necessary to establish strategic costing as an ongoing tool in assessing your, and any, company's viability, both present and future.

Strategic costing enables you to:

- Know your company's, your suppliers', and your competitors' product offerings and the processes by which they are produced.
- Understand your suppliers' and your competitors' processes.
- Establish the actual costs of your company's product and estimate your suppliers' and competitors' costs.
- Compare the variance between target and actual costs, and make changes to the existing production process to obtain target costs and reach optimal performance.
- Determine the value of strategic costing to the company through cash flow analysis.
- Enact changes.
- Continuously improve.

The Strategic Costing Process is a high-level evaluation intended to capture the big picture. Be careful not to get caught up in the minutia of each cost category.

To accomplish strategic costing, you can work individually, but a team effort is usually most effective. The team should be multifunctional in order to take advantage of all the expertise the company has to offer. The most effective team includes personnel from manufacturing, engineering, R&D, and sales, in addition to a member from the business unit of interest. But whether implemented by an individual or a team, this process maximizes contribution to the company's bottom line.

A corporation's bottom line (also known as its profits, net income, or after-tax income) is determined by calculating annual revenues or sales, then subtracting the cost of goods sold, operating expenses, and income tax. Net income is the bottom line as shown in Figure 1-1.

For manufacturers, cost of goods sold is the cost of making the products that are sold. Materials are usually a large portion of this cost. For a retailer, wholesaler, or distributor, cost of goods is what the company paid for the products that were sold, as well as associated transportation. Service companies do not have a cost of goods sold. They may either show cost of services provided or simply list the major expenses incurred in providing the service.

To show how effective strategic costing can be, the following two case studies display the process at work.

FIGURE 1-1.
Format for calculating corporate bottom line

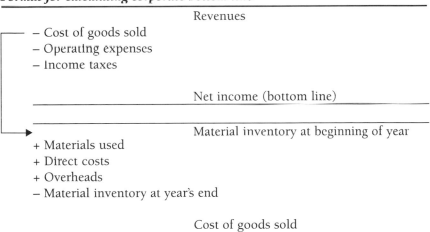

Revenues

– Cost of goods sold
– Operating expenses
– Income taxes

Net income (bottom line)

Material inventory at beginning of year

+ Materials used
+ Direct costs
+ Overheads
– Material inventory at year's end

Cost of goods sold

Case Study: Effect of Reducing Material Costs

Let's travel to ABC Company's manufacturing facility and examine its product F for profitability. ABC's strategic costing team has identified a program for reducing material costs as a way to be more competitive, as well as to improve the bottom line. Examine ABC Company's current profit and loss statement for product F as shown in Figure 1-2.

If ABC Company were able to reduce its materials costs on all items used in product F by half, the resulting effect on the bottom line would be as shown in the revised income statement in Figure 1-3.

The net effect on the bottom line is an increase in net profits of $320,000, or a 32 percent increase!

FIGURE 1-2.
Income statement for product F

Item	Transaction Amount (thousand $)	Balance (thousand $)
Revenues		4,000
– Cost of goods sold	1,900	2,100
– Operating expenses	500	1,600
– Income taxes (40%)	600	
Net income		1,000
Material inventory at beginning of year		1,500
+ Materials used	1,000	
+ Direct costs	800	
+ Overheads	600	
– Material inventory at year's end	2,000	
Cost of goods sold		1,900

FIGURE 1-3.
Income statement for product F after cost reduction

Item	Transaction Amount (thousand $)	Balance (thousand $)
Revenues		4,000
– Cost of goods sold	1,400	2,600
– Operating expenses	500	2,100
– Income taxes (40%)	780	
Net income		1,320
Material inventory at beginning of year		1,500
+ Materials used	500	
+ Direct costs	800	
+ Overheads	600	
– Material inventory at year's end	2,000	
Cost of goods sold		1,400

Case Study: Importance of Reducing Material Costs

Mary B. has recently been promoted to purchasing manager at Crandall Cosmetics. She has been in the purchasing department since graduating with her MBA four years ago. She is very familiar with the company's purchasing policies and its relationships with its suppliers.

During a recent staff meeting the following statistics are presented:

Cost of goods sold equals 75 percent of sales
Materials represent 70 percent of cost of goods sold

Mary also learns at the staff meeting that ten key supplier contracts represent 80 percent of all production procurement dollars.

After the staff meeting Mary reviews Dun & Bradstreet's latest "Industry Norms and Key Business Ratios" and notes that the norm for the cosmetic industry for cost of goods sold as a percentage of sales is 70 percent. Mary surmises that the main reason Crandall's percentage is higher than the norm is that material prices are high.

Mary considers a number of actions that could reduce material costs. She runs several scenarios for reductions in material costs of 5, 10, and 25 percent just to see the effect the changes would have on Crandall's bottom line. Mary's results are staggering and remind her of the power the purchasing department has to affect company profitability. Figure 1-4 shows Mary's calculations.

Crandall Cosmetics' sales last year were $8 million; therefore cost of goods sold was $6 million with the materials portion being $4.2 million. Operating expenses were $500,000, and income taxes were $600,000. If Crandall Cosmetic can identify material reductions of 10 percent, it will realize a quarter-million dollar increase in the bottom line, or a 28 percent increase in net income. A 10 percent reduction in material costs will also bring the company in line with the cosmetic industry norm of cost of goods sold as 70 percent of sales.

Mary looks forward to presenting these data at the next staff meeting. She feels confident that the purchasing department can negotiate a 10 percent material price reduction with Crandall's ten key suppliers.

These two examples show the power strategic costing has to affect the bottom line just by lowering material costs. However, even though the first items usually reviewed in the Strategic Costing Process are materials and supplier costs, it's important to focus on more than one area. To become the "best of the best," you must pay attention to all four steps in strategic costing!

Also, it's important to understand the reasoning behind each step as well as the math fundamentals in order to complete the process successfully. Let's do a quick overview of the four steps before we go into the details that make them work.

FIGURE 1-4.

Reduction in material costs for Crandall Cosmetics

Item	Current (thousand $)	Reduced (thousand $)		
		5% Reduction in Materials	10% Reduction in Materials	25% Reduction in Materials
Sales	8,000	8,000	8,000	8,000
– Cost of goods sold	6,000	5,790	5,580	4,950
– Materials	4,200	3,990	3,780	3,150
– Operating expenses	2,000	2,210	2,420	$3,050
	500	500	500	500
– Taxes (40%)	1,500	1,710	1,920	2,550
	600	684	768	1,020
Net income	900	1,026	1,152	1,530

Step 1: Estimate Supplier Costs

When companies are able to estimate their suppliers' costs, they gain a powerful advantage and can control the purchasing process. Then they are able to take the next step: negotiate lower purchase prices to minimize material costs.

In order to perform this step, a cost model is required that will estimate a supplier's total costs accurately. The model included on the computer disk is the result of six years of study of the correlation factors that drive costs. It has evolved into a relatively simple set of equations. What you need to know about your supplier is the materials, labor, and investment used in the process to make the product or service that you purchase. The model provided can be applied to a myriad of different products and services. It has been validated and shown to come within 10 percent of actual costs: it is a powerful tool for estimation. The equations may be tailored to your particular industry to make the estimates even more accurate. This model can be used with confidence to identify areas for which a lower purchase price can be negotiated.

Step 2: Estimate Competitor Costs

On the surface, estimating competitors' costs might seem impossible. However, you can, using ethical methods, estimate a competitor's costs with the same tool you used to estimate supplier costs. The key information needed is similar for both estimates: materials, labor, and investment. It is much easier to obtain this information for a supplier because you can tour its facility; for a competitor, you'll have to do a little more digging to obtain the information. It is very possible, however, to obtain accurate data about a competitor. And once you have established your competitors' costs, you can compare them with your company's costs in order to study the differences.

Step 3: Set Target Cost and Identify Areas to Improve

Most companies use one of two common methods, coming from two different perspectives, to set product price. The first method calculates the price by totaling actual production or service costs and then tacking on a profit (cost + profit = target price).

The second method begins with the price the market will bear then subtracts the desired profit to arrive at an acceptable production or service cost. Neither method maximizes profits because there is no pressure to reduce costs below what is acceptable to yield the required profit and price.

In order to maximize profits, price should be determined by the marketplace value of the product and cost should be aligned with the competition. By dealing with price and cost independently, a company minimizes costs and maximizes prices and profitability.

To identify areas where company costs can be improved and to recommend programs aimed at reducing costs, first estimate competitor costs and compare them with you company's costs. The variances between the two will indicate where and to what extent improvement is needed. Your company can then develop programs and strategies to improve those areas. When the programs are successful, they can elevate company profitability above the competition.

Step 3 is useful not only for setting and planning strategies for lowering costs, but also for revisiting these plans frequently to make sure your company stays on top and continuously improves.

Step 4: Calculate Value to the Company of the Strategic Costing Process

Implementing a strategic costing program usually requires some company investment. In order to justify the investment, answer the following questions: (1) How much better off will my company be by making this investment to improve its cost picture? (2) What effect will the cost improvement have on my company's market position? The answers can be obtained by calculating how cash flow would change if the programs are implemented successfully. The cash flow calculation should be made every time a new strategy is considered, before it is put into action. The bonus from implementing strategic costing is that it allows a company to determine the market position it will be in.

Aggressive companies use the four-step Strategic Costing Process to evaluate and direct efforts to be competitive, improve continuously, and reach optimal performance. Figure 1-5 summarizes the process.

FIGURE 1-5.
Strategic Costing Process flow chart

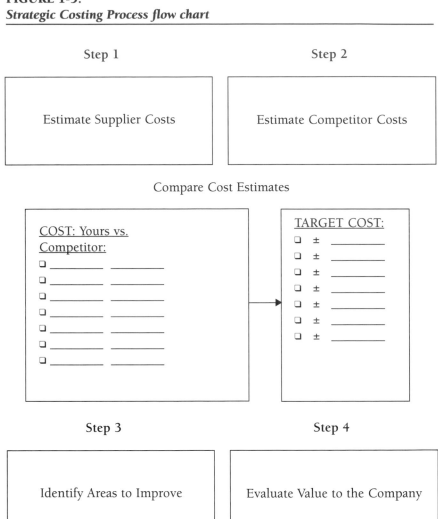

Step 1   Step 2

Estimate Supplier Costs   Estimate Competitor Costs

Compare Cost Estimates

COST: Yours vs.
Competitor:

TARGET COST:

Step 3   Step 4

Identify Areas to Improve   Evaluate Value to the Company

STEP 1:
ESTIMATE
SUPPLIER COSTS

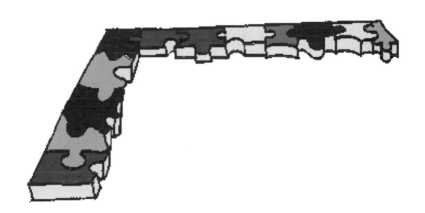

2

PRODUCT COSTS

In 1897, an Italian economist named Pareto discovered that the incomes of individuals are distributed by what has become known as the 80–20 rule. This rule states that 80 percent of the money within an economic system is held by 20 percent of the people. Dr. Joseph Juran first applied this concept to the process improvement area. He discovered that most problems are distributed according to the 80–20 Pareto principle. The same is true for strategic costing; that is, 80 percent of cost can be found in 20 percent of the cost elements. Therefore, a company that concentrates on the areas that have the greatest impact on costs has a better chance of developing a set of equations to estimate the majority of costs. Remember, the model is used to *estimate* supplier and competitor costs, not to calculate actual costs.

Supplier Costs

Though many supplier relationships are moving toward strategic supply alliances, traditional arm's-length supplier relationships still exist. In an arm's-length relationship, the purchaser must discover the main drivers of the supplier's costs in order to demand competitive material pricing. Even within a strategic supply alliance, in which both companies

FIGURE 2-1.
Format for calculating cost of goods sold

                                    Material inventory at beginning of year
+ Materials used
+ Direct costs
+ Overheads
− Material inventory at year's end

                                    Cost of goods sold

---

jointly study costs and their drivers in order to reduce material costs, it is necessary for the purchaser to be aware of the supplier's costs.

When conducting a supplier cost analysis, there are two ways for the purchaser to determine an agreeable cost. It can request a quote from the supplier, or it can estimate supplier costs for itself, which is what you will learn to do in step 1 of the Strategic Costing Process.

Product costs have three main elements: materials used, direct costs, and overheads. Let's begin the analysis by looking at Figure 2-1, the standard accounting formula for calculating cost of goods sold.

To tailor a model to estimate product cost, a few changes must be made to this table. First, completely exclude inventory and expand direct costs to include labor, utilities, maintenance, and depreciation, property taxes, and insurance. Then expand overheads to include both plant and corporate overheads (also called operating expenses and general and administrative costs, respectively). Now the revised product cost table has seven elements and looks like the one shown in Figure 2-2.

Once the seven elements of cost that the supplier will incur are calculated, we can add a profit margin and estimate the supplier's price with reasonable accuracy. Let's look more closely at each cost and the qualifying factors that determine it.

FIGURE 2-2.
Revised product cost table

Item	Amount
Materials used	
Direct costs	
Labor	
Utilities	
Maintenance	
Depreciation, property taxes, and insurance	
Plant overheads	
General and administrative costs	
Total	

Materials Used

Materials used are all the materials that go into the manufacture of a product or subassembly of the final product. An example of a very basic assembly is a mousetrap. The essential materials in a mousetrap are:

Subassemblies	Materials Used
Wooden base	Wood: 3″ × 3″ × 1/4″
Snap spring	Coil steel wire: 1/32″ (outside diameter) × 1 foot long
Hold-down lever	Coil steel wire: 1/32″ × 3″
Holder bracket	Coil steel wire: 1/32″ × 8″
Bait holder	Flat steel: 1/16″ × 1/2″ × 1/2″

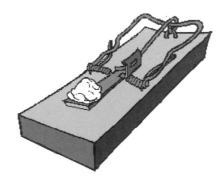

A bill of materials lists all the subassemblies of the final product. The essential material costs are also listed on the bill of materials as seen below:

Bill of Materials: Mousetrap

Item	Quantity	Material Cost
Wooden base	1	$0.25
Snap spring	1	0.03
Hold-down lever	1	0.01
Holder bracket	1	0.01
Bait holder	1	0.02
Total materials cost		$0.32

Essential materials can be as simple as a pound of high-density polyethylene plastic for an injection-molded garbage can, or extremely complex, such as the over 4,000 subassemblies in an automobile.

Essential materials are usually the largest component of cost for a manufacturing product, but they may be almost negligible for a service item.

Direct Costs

Direct costs are costs directly associated with the production of the product or service. The four major direct costs are:

1. Labor
2. Utilities
3. Maintenance
4. Depreciation, property taxes, and insurance

The first component, labor, is self-explanatory. It includes total labor directly associated with the production, assembly, packing, testing, inspection, and shipping of the product or service. If the product is manufactured on a shift basis, total direct labor must include all shifts. Total direct labor is expressed as hours spent.

All other components of direct costs deal with the equipment and facilities used to produce the product or service. For example, if the service is a computer software program, it is produced on a large mainframe computer. The mainframe computer requires electric power to run. It needs to be maintained in order to keep running. The company must pay property taxes based on its value, and it will most likely insure the computer for its replacement value.[1] If the product or service utilizes 100 percent of the equipment or facility, it will carry 100 percent of the utility maintenance, depreciation, property tax, and insurance costs. However, if the product or service only utilizes the equipment or facility a fraction of the time, utility maintenance, depreciation, property tax, and insurance costs should be allocated according to the percentage of utilization.

Plant Overheads

Overhead, or burden costs, include all indirect costs or costs not associated with the direct production of the product or service. In the manufacturing arena all direct costs are associated with the production of a single product and all overheads, or indirect costs, are incurred within the factory but are not associated with only one product or service but with several. Therefore, overhead costs are divided among all products.

Plant overhead cost categories include plant administration, employee relations, medical staff and facilities, fire and plant protection, interplant transportation, communications, engineering assistance to operations, grounds upkeep, and cafeteria.

For service industries overheads are usually only office administration, employee relations, communications, and office upkeep.

---

1. Replacement value is the cost in current dollars to replace a piece of equipment or facility.

The allocation of overhead costs can be critical in determining product strategies. It is discussed at length in Chapter 3.

General and Administrative Costs

"General and administrative costs" are costs incurred from the support functions of the direct and indirect product or service costs. Major categories are selling expenses, R&D expenses, staff department expenses, and shipping costs.

Selling expenses include all costs of personal selling such as salaries, travel and entertainment expenses, commissions, sales office rental, and advertising, sales promotion, and other marketing expenses.

R&D expenses include salaries, lab space costs, and analytical R&D equipment costs.

Staff department expenses include all expenses incurred by legal, finance, engineering, purchasing, accounting, and information systems, and central engineering departments. It includes salaries, office space costs, and clerical expenses.

The last category, shipping, includes all expenses incurred for finished product distribution including freight, finished product warehousing, and storage.

In summary, let me say that I have taught strategic costing techniques for six years with the American Management Association (AMA). At the beginning of every class, I ask participants to call out the major elements of cost for their industries. I usually start with service industries. Invariably participants come up with the seven major elements just discussed. When I query them for the single most important element, they always say the same thing: labor. Participants from manufacturing industries categorize costs in exactly the same way as service industry participants, the only difference being that the single most important cost element in the manufacturing arena is materials. Therefore, the model for estimating costs focuses on seven areas:

1. Materials used
2. Labor
3. Utilities
4. Maintenance
5. Depreciation, property taxes, and insurance
6. Plant overheads
7. General and administrative costs

So far, we have discussed at length the terminology used in the Strategic Costing Process. We're still laying all the puzzle pieces out to see where they fit into the picture. So, now that you know *what* you are looking for, you're ready to find out how to estimate the costs you need for your analysis.

CHAPTER

3

How to Estimate
Product Costs

Estimating supplier or competitor costs is not so cumbersome when you dissect the elements and understand how each one affects product cost. In summarizing thousands of product cost sheets, I have found that 90 to 95 percent of total costs are represented by the seven elements discussed in Chapter 2:

1. Materials used
2. Labor
3. Utilities
4. Maintenance
5. Plant overheads
6. Depreciation, property taxes, and insurance
7. General and administrative costs

While researching these seven cost areas and studying a myriad of available existing product cost sheets, I looked for drivers common to the seven costs. I also used research on common cost factors published in 1980 and updated in January 1998 by the Stanford Research Institute. I was pleased to find that Pareto's law was definitely at work among the major drivers of these seven costs. Three items have the greatest impact on costs: materials used, total investment, and labor. Now the task is to develop factors that when multiplied by these three common drivers result in accurate and reliable estimates. Once this is accomplished, estimating supplier costs and estimating the very elusive competitor costs is far simpler.

This knowledge allows all sorts of wonderful things to happen. Estimating supplier costs yields insight and enables lower material costs to be negotiated. Understanding competitor costs allows them to be compared with your own costs to see where competitors have an advantage or disadvantage. All this information provides a framework within which your company can be more competitive and can establish realistic targets for continuous improvement.

Sound familiar? The Strategic Costing Process brainchild was born through working with these cost sheets! The process of gathering the data to make these cost estimates is usually not trivial, but this necessary investment is time and money wisely spent. A corporation could choose its biggest selling products or services, and apply the strategic costing methodology only to those lines as a first step toward a new level of competitiveness and profitability.

Materials Used

If possible, obtain a bill of materials. If you cannot get one you might have to "reverse engineer" the product. This means that you take the product whose cost you are estimating and disassemble it to determine all the materials your supplier or competitor had to put into the final product as delivered. In the case of liquids—for example, chemicals and perfumes—you could use gas chromatography, which separates all the chemicals used in the final recipe. Once you have a complete list of materials in the product you are estimating, you have to calculate the quantity used per final shipped unit and the material price in dollars per unit or dollars per pound. This number must be divided by the process yield. The process yield adjusts for scrap, or the number of parts that were made (usually more than one) to make one good part. Someone has to pay for this wasted material, and it's always the customer.

The equation for material cost is material price times quantity produced (units) divided by yield. It looks like this:

$$\text{Materials used} = \text{Price} \times (\text{Units/Yield})$$

Let's see this equation in action!

Case Study: Materials Used at Laser Company

The vice president of engineering at Laser Company is given the task of identifying areas of improvement for a laser probe, one of many products produced by the company. He feels that material costs are probably high for the probe, but nobody at Laser Company really knows for sure. Bill Y., an industrial engineer, is given the assignment to calculate material costs for the probe. The probe sells for $600, and everyone believes that materials probably make up a high percentage of the costs to produce the probe. Bill is to quantify the probe material costs, so the first thing he does is put together a bill of materials, which looks like this:

Bill of Materials: Laser Probe
Fiber optic cable:	2 feet
Flex tube (plastic):	2 feet
Spring action mechanism	
Laser cutters:	2 units

Bill knows that 3,500 probes are assembled yearly. He calculates the composite cost using the strategic costing equation for estimating materials: $P \times (U/Y)$. His calculation is shown in Figure 3-1. Dividing the cost of $1,162,861 by 3,500 salable probes gives material costs per probe of $332.25.

FIGURE 3-1.
Calculation of material costs for Laser Company

Materials	Unit Price ($)	Quantity Used	Yield (%)	Annual Costs ($)
Fiber optic cable	75.00	3,500	90	291,667
Flex tube	5.00	3,500	95	18,421
Spring action mechanism	22.00	3,500	100	77,000
Laser cutters (2)	215.00	3,500	97	775,773
Total annual costs				$1,162,861

Case Study: Materials Used at Barnes Chemical

Susan B., a chemist at Barnes Chemical, is asked to establish the costs of the materials used to manufacture one million pounds of fiber B per year. First she has to calculate the total quantity of materials used. She does this by multiplying the quantity of material per pound of fiber by the one million pounds produced each year. After talking with plant operations personnel about material yields, she puts together the material cost sheet shown in Figure 3-2.

Labor

To estimate yearly labor cost you need to know two things: the total number of people working directly on the product or service and their average wage rate.

The number of people working directly on the product or service may be obtained by actually counting them during a tour of your supplier's plant. You could also just ask outright or make an educated guess.

The average wage rate may be obtained by asking the local chamber of commerce for its average regional pay scale. Again,

FIGURE 3-2.
Calculation of material costs for fiber B

	Unit Price ($/lb)	Quantity per Pound of Fiber	Fiber Sold (million lb)	Quantity Used (million lb)	Yield (%)	Annual Costs ($)
Solvent	2	.25	1	.25	75	666,666
Glycol	2	.75	1	.75	80	1,875,000
Additives	5	.10	1	.10	95	526,315
Stabilizers	20	.05	1	.05	90	900,000
Total annual costs						3,967,981
Material costs per pound of fiber B						3.97

you could also just ask your supplier's facility tour guide. It's amazing what people know and are willing to share with you if you simply ask.

Once you have an estimate of the number of people working directly on the product or service and their pay scale, escalating that information to an annual labor cost will require multiplying the information by four factors that adjust for vacation, relief, benefits, and supervision.

Vacation Factor

Employees are entitled to paid vacations, and thus this time must be included in the yearly labor cost calculation, because while an operator is on paid vacation, another person must be paid to perform the operation or service. We assume an average of three weeks paid vacation and eleven paid holidays, which is twenty-six days, or 208 hours. Assuming one shift of operations, there are 2,080 hours in a year (8 hours per day times 5 per week times 52 weeks per year). Subtracting 208 from 2,080 and dividing that number into 2,080 gives a vacation multiplying factor of 1.11:

Hours/Year – Vacation and holiday = Total hours worked
2,080 – 208 = 1,872
2,080/1,872 = 1.11

Relief Factor

The relief factor builds in some cost to compensate for less than 8 hours of production in an 8-hour day. Operators take lunch, rest room breaks, and communication breaks throughout the day. They are paid for 8 hours, but actually only work on average 6.5 hours per day. The relief multiplying factor is thus 1.23 (8 divided by 6.5).

Benefits Factor

Employees are entitled to health care benefits. These amount to about 30 percent of their base pay and need to be included in a yearly labor cost calculation. Therefore, the benefits multiplier is 1.3.

Supervision Factor

An adjustment for first-line supervision should be included in an annual labor cost calculation. We assume one first-line supervisor for every ten operators. The supervisor is paid at a higher rate than the operators, so the multiplier to account for first-line supervision is 1.3.

An accurate estimate of annual labor costs is number of people, times average wage rate, times total hours worked in a year,[1] times vacation, relief, benefits, and supervision factors. The equation looks like this:

No. of operators $\times$ Wage rate $\times$ 2,080 $\times \underbrace{(1.11*1.23*1.3*1.3)}$

Approximately 4,800

Case Study: Labor Used to Produce Scanning Instruments

Mark has worked as a buyer for St. Michael's Hospital for twenty-four years. He has always taken pride in providing the

---

1. If the product or service is produced in less than a year, this number would be the actual hours required.

hospital staff with the finest quality products available. In a recent group meeting, Mark's superiors discussed how St. Michael's Hospital would be evolving into a profit-making organization at the beginning of the next year.

To prepare for this change, Mark's boss requests that he analyze two suppliers of scanning instruments prior to St. Michael's purchasing 200 of these units to be used throughout the hospital. Comparable units have been selling for approximately $4,500.

Mark is very excited about this new challenge for the purchasing department. The department will play a vital role in making sure St. Michael's makes a profit on all its purchases. Mark's strategy for getting the best price on the scanning instruments is first to check with the finance department to determine the maximum affordable price, next to visit each supplier to estimate its costs, and then, using strategic costing calculations to guide him, to negotiate the best deal for St. Michael's Hospital.

His visit to the finance department is a little shocking. They state that in order to earn a slight profit at the end of three years (the predetermined life of the units), the maximum affordable price for the instruments is $5,000. Recent quotes from two suppliers, for a quantity of 200, are $5,150 and $5,400 per unit.

Next Mark sets up a visit to each supplier's plant, asking two of his friends, one from engineering and one from accounting, to join him on the tours. Mark wants to determine each supplier's labor costs because he believes that the assembly of the scanning instruments is probably very labor intensive and his estimate of labor costs is therefore critical. He asks both his friends to count the people they see during the tours, both the ones assembling the instruments and the people who appear to be transporting or inspecting the units.

After the two very informative tours, Mark compares his operator count with those made by his friends. Each supplier works on a two-shift basis, so the numbers they count are multiplied by two. One supplier appears to be considerably more automated. The labor counts are listed in Figure 3-3.

FIGURE 3-3.
Labor counts for St. Michael's suppliers

Supplier	Mark's	Engineering	Accounting	Average
A	52	56	48	52
B	34	32	32	32

Some workers appear to be doing multiple operations and still others are working on several completely different products during the day. This observation tends to make the tallies a little difficult, but you can see that the deviation among Mark and his friends from engineering and accounting is not great for either plant.

Mark next calculates total labor costs for each supplier. He checks at the local chamber of commerce for average assembly worker wages in each supplier's area. The average wage rate for supplier A is $17.50 per hour and for supplier B is $21.00 per hour.

Each supplier produces 1,000 instruments per shift per year, so they each could produce the 200 instruments that St. Michael's would order using only 10 percent of total yearly labor:

200/(1,000 instruments/shift/year $\times$ 2 shifts/day) = .1 (10%)

Mark's labor calculations for each supplier are shown in Figure 3-4.

Mark was correct! The labor costs for the scanning machines are considerable. Of its $5,400 price tag, supplier A's labor costs are $2,184 per unit ($436,800 divided by 200 instruments). Supplier B is indeed more automated, so Mark is a little puzzled at this point as to why its price is $5,150 when its labor costs are only $1,613 per unit ($322,560 divided by 200 instruments).

Mark now feels ready to begin negotiations with each supplier to try to reduce the price per instrument and enable St. Michael's Hospital to obtain its desired profit. Because of his efforts, he is able to secure a quote for the 200 instruments from supplier B at a cost of $4,650 per unit.

FIGURE 3-4.
Calculation of labor for St. Michael's suppliers

Supplier	Equation	Annual Labor Costs
A	52 × $17.50 × 4,800 × 10%	$436,800
B	32 × $21.00 × 4,800 × 10%	$322,560

Utilities

Utilities include all the power associated with running the equipment used to produce the product. This power can be electricity, steam, hydraulic energy, and so on. All utilities are based on the equipment used and are therefore driven by investment in that equipment. As with the other costs, I studied thousands of cost sheets for a myriad of products ranging from fibers, injection-molded parts, assemblies, instruments, and small precision powder metal parts. Using total investment as the driver, I analyzed for the percentage of investment that provides a good estimate of annual utility costs. This percentage turned out to be 2 percent. Although the percentage had a fairly wide standard deviation, 2 percent was indeed the mean, as seen in Figure 3-5.

The number that represents total investment is the total replacement investment for the equipment used plus the investment needed to install the equipment. You need not only to estimate what it would cost to buy the equipment new but also to multiply it by three to include installation, project management, and facilities associated with getting the equipment ready to run. In estimating a supplier's equipment investment it's always wise to take someone from engineering along on a visit to your supplier. That individual can recognize which equipment is being used to produce the product and can either estimate the equipment's new value or request a quote from the vendor of the equipment. The vendor's name is always prominently displayed on any major piece of equipment.

FIGURE 3-5.
Annual utility costs vs. percentage of total investment

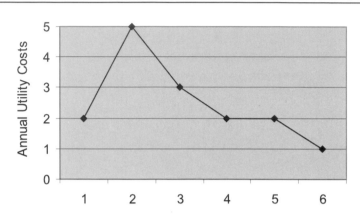

% of Total Investment

For example, when I estimated the annual utility costs for a thousand-ton injection molding press made by Cincinnati Milacron, I first requested a vendor quote. Their quote was $250,000, which is the replacement investment.

I then multiplied the replacement investment by three to account for installation and facilities (power, lighting, and heating or air conditioning) for a total investment of $750,000. This is the number that drives the estimate for utilities. (The investment driver is also used to estimate maintenance and depreciation, so taking the time to develop a good-quality investment number is well worth the effort.)

To calculate the annual utility cost, take 2 percent of total investment. In the example of the thousand-ton press annual utilities would be:

$$\text{Utilities} = \text{Total investment} \times .02$$
$$= \$750,000 \times .02$$
$$= \$15,000 \text{ per year}$$

If the injection molding press is used only a portion of the year, the annual utility cost would be multiplied by the portion of the year the equipment is actually being used. In our previous example, if the injection molding press is used to manufacture parts that your company purchases and those parts can be made in 1/10th of the year, the utility cost that concerns you is 1/10th the annual utility cost, or $1,500.

Maintenance

Maintenance includes both the labor and the materials needed to keep the process that is making the product or service, such as a mainframe computer, maintained and producing in an efficient manner. This element of cost is directly related to investment in the equipment used. Annual maintenance costs are estimated at 6 percent of the total investment.

$$\text{Maintenance} = .06 \times \text{Total investment}$$

On a recent trip to Japan, I had a discussion with a maintenance contract firm. Most Japanese companies do not have their own maintenance staffs but rather rely on contract firms. I asked, "How do you determine your contract quote?" The response was that they estimate replacement investment and take 6 percent of that for an annual contract quote. I was very interested to note the similarity between my estimating factor and the actual measure used by a Japanese maintenance contract firm.

Plant Overheads

Overheads include all the indirect costs associated with the production of the product or service. This term encompasses many different elements, depending on the company and the industrial sector. Let me define what I include in overhead. If your company, and therefore your supplier or competitor, includes something different, you will have to adjust this formula to estimate overheads accordingly. The items included are:

■ General plant burden
■ Overtime

- Plant administration (management and staff)
- Employee relations
- Medical staff and facilities
- Fire and plant protection
- Interplant transportation (shipping and receiving)
- Carrying and acquisition costs
- Communications
- Computers and telephone systems
- Engineering assistance to operations
- Grounds upkeep
- Cafeteria

The problem with assigning or allocating overhead costs to a product or service when more than one product or service is produced at a given location is defining a correct method to distribute the costs.

Case Study: Overhead Allocation Dilemma at PDQ Machinery

Bill White, a recent MBA graduate, has been assigned the task of estimating supplier overheads by looking at PDQ Machinery's overheads and applying percentage of labor as the criterion for distribution. The first thing Bill does is visit the accounting office and ask for overheads for the three products PDQ manufactures. He is given a copy of last year's cost data for the three products, along with total overhead charges. The total overhead breakdown is:

Engineering	$15,000
Overtime	2,000
Plant administration	15,000
Carrying costs	1,000
Telephone	1,000
Packing	3,000
Shipping and receiving	2,000
Overhead subtotal	$39,000

For years PDQ has allocated overheads using the volume of each product as a guide. For example, product C, which has 57.1 percent of total plant volume, has traditionally picked up 57.1 percent of overhead charges, as in Figure 3-6.

Bill is interested in product C because the supplier whose overheads he has been asked to estimate supplies the raw materials for product C. When Bill estimates the overheads of PDQ as a function of labor, his calculation is as shown in Figure 3-7.

Bill realizes that this way of allocating overhead charges could be erroneous. It takes a lot of work, but Bill collects the data necessary to allocate overhead charges using activity-based costing, as in Figure 3-8.[2] New calculations of overheads as a percentage of labor are shown in Figure 3-9.

This case study shows the power of allocating overheads according to activity-based costing and using that figure to calculate supplier overheads. We would suggest that you do this kind of allocation of overhead charges and make the calculation as a percentage of labor. This will be a good estimate of supplier overheads. However, if you cannot get this kind of data, a good formula for estimating overheads that include the factors listed above is:

$$\text{Overheads} = .75 \times \text{Labor}$$

Depreciation, Property Taxes, and Insurance

Depreciation is one of the most misunderstood concepts associated with both the cost sheet and cash flow analysis. Depreciation is an accounting element, a "noncash cost" in total costs. It is basically an incentive the government gives to corporations to encourage them to continue to invest. Fixed assets in which a company invests have a "useful life," which is usually ten years. The investment depreciation each year is thus 10 percent of the replacement value of the facility (equip-

---

2. *Activity-based costing* is a system to allocate costs by breaking down an organization into activities. An activity is to convert resources into outputs. Activity accounting identifies activities performed and determines their costs.

FIGURE 3-6.
Overhead allocation by volume

	A	B	C
Volume	10,000	5,000	20,000
Volume as a % of total	28.6%	14.3%	57.1%
Price, $	$5.00	$10.00	$2.50
Sales, $	$50,000	$50,000	$50,000
Costs:			
Materials	$1.00	$2.00	$0.50
Labor	$1.25	$2.70	$0.60
Power, Taxes and Ins.	$0.05	$0.10	$0.05
Maintenance	$0.30	$0.40	$0.15
Subtotal Costs:	$2.60	$5.20	$1.30

Overheads:			
Engineering	$15,000		
Overtime	$2,000		
Plant Administration	$15,000		
Carrying Costs	$1,000		
Telephone	$1,000		
Packing	$3,000		
Shipping and Receiving	$2,000		
Overhead Subtotal:	$39,000		

Overhead Allocated by Volume:	$11,154	$5,577	$22,269
Unit Overhead Costs:	$1.12	$1.12	$1.11
Total Costs:	$3.72	$6.32	$2.41
Before Tax Profit:	$1.28	$3.68	$0.09
Percent	26%	37%	3%

FIGURE 3-7.
Calculation of overhead for product C

Overhead of product C = $22,269 (= $39,000 × 57.1%)
Labor costs for product C = $12,000 (= 20,000 units × $.60/unit for labor)
Overhead as a percentage of labor = $22,269/$12,000 = 186%

FIGURE 3-8.
Overhead allocation by activity-based costing

		A	B	C
Volume		10,000	5,000	20,000
Volume as a % of total		28.6%	14.3%	57.1%
Price, $		$5.00	$10.00	$2.50
Sales, $		$50,000	$50,000	$50,000
Costs:				
Materials		$1.00	$2.00	$0.50
Labor		$1.25	$2.70	$0.60
Power,Taxes and Ins.		$0.05	$0.10	$0.05
Maintenance		$0.30	$0.40	$0.15
Subtotal Costs:		$2.60	$5.20	$1.30
Overheads:	based on:			
Engineering	work orders	$3,750	$5,250	$6,000
Overtime	product requests	$0	$1,500	$500
Plant Administration	plant staff	$2,000	$10,000	$3,000
Carrying Costs	warehousing costs	$250	$250	$500
Telephone	actual usage	$250	$250	$500
Packing	area activity	$1,000	$500	$1,500
Shipping and Receiving	area activity	$500	$500	$1,000
Overhead Subtotal:		$7,750	$18,250	$13,000
Unit Overhead Costs:		$0.78	$3.65	$0.65
Total Costs:		$3.38	$8.85	$1.95
Before Tax Profit:		$1.63	$1.15	$0.55
Percent		33%	12%	22%

FIGURE 3-9.
Calculation of overhead for product C based on activity-based costing

Overhead of product C = $13,000
Labor costs for product C = $12,000
Overhead as a percentage of labor = $13,000/$12,000 = 108%

ment and building), assuming ten years of useful life. Therefore, the equation used to estimate investment depreciation is:

$$\text{Depreciation} = .10 \times \text{Total investment}$$

To this calculation we add property taxes and insurance on the
facility at 1 percent, and the final equation is:

$$\text{Depreciation, property taxes, and insurance}$$
$$= .11 \times \text{Total investment}$$

General and Administrative Costs

Typical general and administrative costs are common costs
for the entire community. They include:

- Selling expenses[3]
- Executive compensation
- R&D expenses
- Staff department expenses
  Legal
  Finance
  Purchasing
  Accounting
  Information systems
  Central engineering
- Office space
- Clerical
- Shipping expenses

Allocating these expenses is even harder than allocating
overheads and is probably not worth the effort. You can take
annual reports for your company, your suppliers, and your competitors and, as a rule of thumb, calculate general and adminis-

---

3. Selling expenses include all costs of personal selling such as salaries, travel and entertainment expenses, commissions, sales office rental, and advertising, sales promotion, and other
marketing expenses.

FIGURE 3-10.
Income statement for Steadman Company

Item	Transaction Amount	Balance
Revenue		$4,500
– Cash expenses	2,500	
– G&A expenses	500	
– Depreciation	500	
Pretax income		1,000
– Income taxes (40%)	400	
Net income		$600

trative costs as a percentage of all expenses. This will usually be around 15 percent of the total of all costs. For example, assume the data from the Steadman Company income statement shown in Figure 3-10.

Here total expenses (cash expenses and depreciation) are $3,000 and general and administrative costs are $500, or 14 percent of total expenses. If you have access to this kind of information (which can be found in a company's annual report), calculate actual general and administrative costs as a percentage of total expenses, and use that calculation when you are estimating total costs. If this information is not available, a good estimate for general and administrative costs is 15 percent of total expenses. Therefore, the equation to estimate general and administrative costs is:

General and administrative costs = .15 × Total expenses

Profit

Suppliers must earn a reasonable profit or they will go out of business and a source of materials for your process could dry up. Whenever negotiating with a supplier on costs never mention profits as an area to cut. Plenty of other areas to cut are identified in Chapter 6. There are several sources for profit and margin ratios, based on industrial sector. Some sources are *The Wall Street Journal*, *Investor's Business Daily*, Robert Morris Associates, and my favorite, Dun & Bradstreet's "Industry Norms and Key Business Ratios." With profit calculated as a percentage of total costs, you will be able to take your calculations to the point where you obtain a price for the supplier's goods or services.

Case Study: Widget International

You request a quote from Widget International for 500,000 widgets. You know that to be competitive you must pay under $4. Each widget weighs one pound, and you estimate their cost using these data (assume a 10 percent markup):

Material price:	$1/lb
Process yield:	90%
Operators needed:	4 (one shift) at $15/hour
Total investment:	$2,000,000

Widget International has quoted a price per widget of $4.13. Use Figure 3-11 to do your own calculations before looking at our estimate for this case study (in Figure 3-12).

Now use the cost-estimating spreadsheet on the disk to estimate a cost for the 500,000 widgets. This is a very accurate estimating spreadsheet based on industry factors. Open up the Cost of Sales spreadsheet by double clicking on the icon. Total costs are calculated automatically. You have only to input your best estimates of the number of operators, their hourly rate, the total material price, the volume of items expected to sell, the total investment, and the product yield. Yield is determined by estimating how many items will be bad or scrap in a lot of 100. For example, if 10 out of 100 are bad, the yield is 90 percent, or 90 good parts divided by 100 made. The spreadsheet opens to an example for Widget International. Just ignore these data and place your own in the boxes. The spreadsheet automatically calculates the total costs in dollars per year and dollars per piece.

FIGURE 3-11.
Cost-estimating table

TOTAL MATERIALS USED		
P x (U/y) [Price per unit quantity times (# ordered times weight divided by yield)]		
UTILITIES		
TI x .02 [Total investment times 2%]		
LABOR		
# x $ x 4800 [Number of operators times hourly rate times 4800]		
MAINTENANCE		
TI x .06 [Total investment times 6%]		
OVERHEADS		
L x .75 [Labor times 75%]		
DEPRECIATION, TAXES, & INSURANCE		
TI x .11 [Total Investment times 11%]		
Subtotal #1		
GENERAL & ADMINISTRATIVE		
Subtotal #1 x .15		
Subtotal #2		
PROFIT		
Subtotal #2 x PM [Subtotal #2 times % estimated profit margin]		
Final Price		
Selling Price/Item [Final price divided by the number to be manufactured]		

FIGURE 3-12.
Cost estimate for Widget International

PROJECTED TOTAL COSTS, of

Widget International

COS, © 1989, Dale Brethauer

BASIC PREMISES:

Number of Operators:	**4**
Hourly Wage Rate:	**$15.00**
Material Price:	**$1.00**
Process Yield:	**90%**
Sales Volume:	**500,000**
Total Investment:	**$2,000,000**

	$/YEAR	$/PIECE
VARIABLE COST		
Materials	**$555,556**	**$1.11**
Utilities	**$40,000**	**$0.08**
Subtotal Variable Costs	**$595,556**	**$1.19**
FIXED COSTS		
Labor	**$287,958**	**$0.58**
Equipment Maintenance	**$120,000**	**$0.24**
Overhead	**$215,969**	**$0.43**
Property Taxes and Insurance	**$20,000**	**$0.04**
Equipment Allocations	**$200,000**	**$0.40**
Subtotal Fixed Costs	**$843,927**	**$1.69**
SUBTOTAL VARIABLE AND FIXED COSTS	**$1,439,482**	**$2.88**
GENERAL AND ADMINISTRATIVE COSTS		
Selling Expense	**$71,974**	**$0.14**
Administration	**$71,974**	**$0.14**
Distribution	**$71,974**	**$0.14**
TOTAL COSTS	**$1,655,405**	**$3.31**

After you have made all your inputs, go up to the file pull-down menu, click once, go down to Save As, and release the mouse button. Give your spreadsheet a name. This action saves the file you just created. You may modify or change it at any date. Remember to save all changes. If you would like to print this document again, go up to the file pull-down menu, go down to Print, and release. This document has already been sized for optimal viewing. Your spreadsheet should look like Figure 3-12.

Summary of Equations

For easy reference Figure 3-13 summarizes the cost-estimating equations.

FIGURE 3-13.
Summary of equations

Category	Equation	Legend
Materials used	$P \times (U/Y)$	P = Price
		U = Unit
		Y = Yield
Utilities	$TI \times .02$	TI = Total investment
Labor	$\# \times \$ \times 4,800$	# = Number of operators
		$ = Hourly rate
Maintenance	$TI \times .06$	TI = Total investment
Plant overheads	$L \times .75$	L = Labor
Depreciation, property taxes, and insurance	$TI \times .11$	TI = Total investment
General and administrative costs	$.15 \times$ Total expenses	

CHAPTER

4

A TOUR OF YOUR
SUPPLIER'S FACILITY

Much good data with which to estimate supplier cost can be obtained by touring your supplier's facility, observing, and asking the right questions. Remember, to estimate supplier costs, you need to know the materials used in making the product, the total number of operators working on the product, and the total investment for all the equipment directly used in the production process.

I suggest forming a team to tour your supplier's facility. This team should include at least three people and involve one from each of three key departments: engineering, purchasing, and manufacturing. Before the tour, the team members should get together to determine the role each will take and the area of focus. Assign each person one of the three main cost drivers—materials used, total investment, and labor—about which to get as much information as possible.

Since the person from the engineering department is probably the most familiar with equipment, he or she is usually assigned to tally all the equipment used to make the product, the vendors of that equipment, and any replacement investments the tour guide knows of. To estimate total investment, the engineering person should make a process flow diagram and list all the major equipment associated with the manufacture of the product. This list of equipment can later be verified and quotes requested from the vendors. Usually, suppliers are particularly proud of any special equipment they use to make their products, and the tour guide will likely be more than willing to disclose any investment numbers he or she knows. In fact, the supplier is a fount of knowledge about its process, and well-thought-out questions posed to the tour guide can go a long way to helping you to understand the production and ultimately supplier costs.

The purchasing person is assigned to get a good understanding of the materials used in making the product. The materials used to manufacture the product can be determined by buying the product and taking it apart (reverse engineering) prior to your tour. This procedure will familiarize the purchasing person with the essential materials used in the product and so increase his or her awareness of these materials and potential scrap or waste as the plant tour is occurring.

The manufacturing person is usually the "people counter." He or she is most familiar with manufacturing operations and can understand the process flow and the people associated with the production process.

The preparatory meeting should be used to discuss roles, questions to ask, and methods to use in order to gain a better understanding of the materials, total investment, and labor used by the supplier.

Consensus Estimation

The estimate of the number of operators directly associated with the production of the product will be more accurate if everyone who goes on the supplier tour makes an individual estimate. Each team member on the tour counts the people encountered during the tour, and the team as a whole comes up with a consensus estimate when the tour has been completed. A consensus estimate of the total number of operators usually yields a number very close to the actual value.

In six years of conducting seminars with the AMA, I have taught a weighted average technique for reaching a consensus decision. I have asked hundreds of groups to estimate the current value of gold in dollars per troy ounce. From everyone I ask for a silent guess on a small piece of paper and an assessment of their expertise in this area. If they have absolutely no ideas, they are assigned to group 1. If they have noticed the price of gold in the newspaper within the past year or are active traders they are assigned to group 3. Anybody with a slight knowledge would then be in group 2. Once the groups are assigned the silent votes are collected and scribed on an easel at the front of the room. The figures are written in three columns, corresponding to the three groups. Each column is totaled; then the column 1 total is multiplied by one, the column 2 total by two, and the column 3 total by three. This method gives more weight to the guesses in group 3. These are the people with the most expertise, so you want their guesses to have more influence on the final average. The three column totals are then totaled, and this figure is divided by the number of guesses made (this is calculated by adding the number of guesses in column 1, two times the number of guesses in column 2, and three times the number of guesses in column 3). The final number is the group's estimate of the current price of gold. In six years of running this exercise the estimates have varied from the actual current price by 1 to 7 percent but never more than 7 percent. This accuracy shows the power of a weighted average consensus estimate. Figure 4-1 shows a recent consensus decision from a group of seventeen people who were attending my class.

On November 12, 1997, when this estimate was made, the price of gold was actually $307. This group came within $19 of the actual price, or within 6 percent. I'd call that a good estimate, and it's one of the more inaccurate estimates that has been made in six years of presenting this technique.

This technique can be used for making many kinds of estimates; here you can use it to estimate the number of operators involved with a production process. The manufacturing person, who has primary responsibility for counting operators, would be the "expert," and his or her guess would be multiplied by three. The other people on the tour could make estimates, but their counts would only be multiplied by one or two.

FIGURE 4-1.
Weighted average consensus for price of gold
_____

First, total the guesses for each group and multiply by the corresponding weights:

Group 1	Group 2	Group 3
$35.00	$ 320.00	$ 310.00
100.00	375.00	305.00
200.00	325.00	308.00
1.50	400.00	305.00
50.00	250.00	
400.00	300.00	
	400.00	
$786.50	$2,370.00	$1,228.00
× 1	× 2	× 3
$786.50	$4,740.00	$3,684.00

Next, add the three columns:

$ 786.50
4,740.00
3,684.00
_____
$9,210.00

Now, calculate the total number of guesses:

Group 1: 6 × 1 = 6
Group 2: 7 × 2 = 14
Group 3: 4 × 3 = 12
Total   32

The estimate for the current price of gold is:
$9,210.00/32 = $288

Plant Tour

I think we're ready now for the tour of our supplier's facility. This supplier is your sole source of powder metal bushings. These bushings are a vital part in the assembly of jet engines. The tolerances are small, and quality is of the utmost importance. You have selected two people from your company to join you, to assist in the collection of data concerning materials used, labor, and total investment. You have had a pretour meeting and discussed everyone's roles and potential questions to ask. You have purchased the product and reverse engineered it. You are prepared for the tour.

Case Study: Powder Metal Inc.'s Facility

Mike   Brad   Amy   Susan

Mike is the plant manager of Powder Metal Inc. He will guide the tour through the powder metal bushing facility.

Susan is the senior buyer for Engine Inc. and is responsible for settling on a price and supplier for next year's order of 50,000 high-precision powder metal bushings. She has received three quotes for the bushings, and Powder Metal Inc.'s price appears fair but is not the lowest bid. She has determined from other buyers that Powder Metal Inc. stands by the quality of its products and is very customer oriented.

Amy is the senior project engineer of Engine Inc. Amy has been with Engine Inc. for five years and has an extensive personal catalog of metal manufacturing equipment and current vendor lists.

Brad is the engine foreman of Engine Inc. and has been with the company for ten years. He has nineteen years' previous experience in the aerospace industry and is very knowledgeable about manufacturing processes.

The tour begins in Mike's office.

Mike: Good afternoon and welcome to Powder Metal Inc. We are very interested in being your supplier of high-precision powder metal bushings and are pleased that you have taken the opportunity to visit our facility.

Susan: Thank you Mike, for your gracious offer of a tour of your facility this afternoon. I have brought with me Amy, our senior project engineer, and Brad, our engine foreman. Brad is well aware of the critical nature of the powder metal bushings for our engines.

Mike: I'd like to welcome all of you here, and I hope this tour and meeting can be beneficial to us all. Please feel free to ask questions about anything you don't understand, and if I don't have the answers, I'll be sure to find someone who does.

Brad: Thanks, Mike. If you could take us through your facility just as if we were the bushing, or in other words, go through each process step in its proper sequence, I believe it would help our understanding immensely.

Mike: I'll be glad to, Brad. Let me start with a few words before we go into the plant. As you know, the high-precision bushing has a final weight of two pounds and an inside diameter accurate to within .0003.

Mike sketches the final bushing dimensions on the white board behind him.

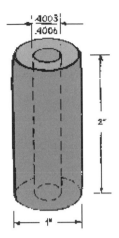

Mike: We start with two pounds of powder metal and two pounds of solvent, which is driven off during the curing operation.

Susan: Mike, do you mean that there are two essential materials that make up the powder metal bushing and that the mixture is 50 percent powder metal and 50 percent solvent?

Mike: That's exactly right, Susan. The solvent is all driven off during curing, so the final product is all powder metal and it weighs two pounds. However, the beginning mixture is two pounds of powder metal and two pounds of solvent.

Susan: I think I understand. Do you try to reclaim the solvent in the operation?

Mike: No, it is all driven off during curing and taken out of the airstream by a scrubber system before the air is vented into the atmosphere.

Susan: Mike, how much do you pay for the powder metal?

Mike: It's fairly expensive because we don't buy in large bulk. We are currently paying about $25 per pound.

Susan: And how much is the solvent?

Mike: The solvent is DMAC, and we pay $2 per pound. The process we are going to see has only been in operation for two years, so everything is fairly new, and we are still working to increase our product yields.

Brad: What are your current yields?

Mike: They are fairly low, I'm sorry to say. Last month we were running about 86 percent yield, but we have an active process improvement team looking into programs to increase efficiency.

Brad: Does that man that you throw out 14 bushings for every hundred ones you ship?

Mike: That's right. We are very proud of the final quality of our bushing and will not ship final product unless it meets a rigid inspection.

Brad: Is there any way to reclaim or recycle the semi-finished or finished product?

Mike: Unfortunately, we can't. Since one of the first process steps drives the solvent off and the powder metal is compacted, the product has almost no recycle value, because at that point a reclaimer would have to reconvert it to powder, which is very expensive. Okay, if there are no further questions we'll begin the tour. Does everyone have a pair of safety glasses?

Susan, Brad, and Amy: We're all set.

Amy: Just one more question before our tour. How many bushings can you manufacture on the line we are going to see?

Mike: That's a good question. Last year we ran two shifts and were able to produce 100,000 powder metal bushings.

Susan: Well, if we ordered 50,000 would you put on a third shift?

Mike: Oh, sure, because an order of 50,000 could almost exactly be manufactured in one shift. Anything else? Okay, follow me and let's start where we receive the essential materials at our receiving dock and from there we'll proceed through the process.

Mike, Susan, Brad, and Amy proceed to the receiving area.

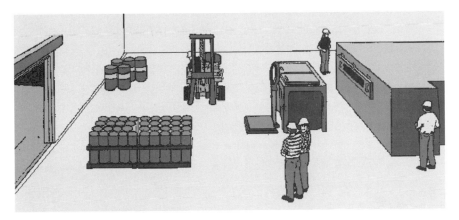

Mike: This is the receiving area. Notice the pallets of powder metal and solvent. The two materials are mixed together and blended in the blend/weigh station. Each cavity of the mold is filled and placed into the oven on trays.

Brad: Excuse me, Mike. I see five people in this area. Are they all associated with this process?

Mike: Well, not exactly. The man in the striped shirt is our area foreman. One person is the forklift driver. He services the entire plant but spends the majority of his time with this process, mostly moving inventory. The other three people are a weighing operator and two oven operators.

Brad: Is the weighing equipment very expensive?

Mike: I'm not really sure, but I don't think so. However, the oven is pretty expensive.

Amy: About how much was it when you purchased it?

Mike: As I recall, it was about $750,000. That included the oven and the scrubber system for the removal of the solvent before venting the airstream to the atmosphere. Are there any other questions before we proceed? Okay, then, this is the end of the oven. Over against the wall you can see some in-process inventory. To your far right is the high-pressure and -temperature press.

Amy: Wow, that press is pretty impressive! Do you know the manufacturer? That must be about as expensive as the oven, and just out of curiosity how much does it take to maintain the press?

Mike: You're very observant, Amy. That press was almost $750,000, the same as the oven. The manufacturer of the press is Cincinnati Milacron, and we spent about 2 percent of the investment, per year, on maintenance.

Mike, Susan, Amy, and Brad proceed past the oven.

Brad: Mike, are those the same operators we saw earlier, at the oven?

Mike: Yes, and we saw the forklift operator before, too. However, the two press operators are new, and there is one more person in the rear of the press whom we'll see in a minute.

Once the bushings come out of the press they go to the quality assurance section of our facility, which is operated by three people.

Amy: Mike, you have mentioned how proud you are of your quality control. Is the instrumentation in this area very expensive?

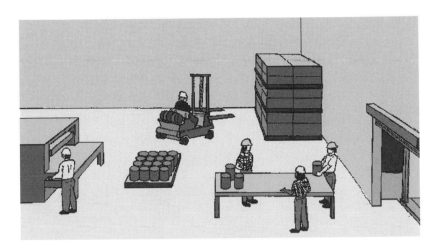

Mike: As a matter of fact, Amy, it was. We have over $250,000 worth of testing equipment, so we can guarantee and stand behind all our bushings.

Susan: Well, that's great, Mike, because you know this bushing will be going into our jet engines and quality is extremely important.

Mike: Well, that's our facility in a nutshell. Would you like to see anything else?

Susan: No, Mike, this has been most informative. We appreciate your time.

Mike: My pleasure.

Amy and Brad: Thanks a lot, Mike.

And so ends the tour of Powder Metal Inc.'s facility. Let's see whether Susan has enough data to make a cost estimate for the powder metal bushings.

Back at Engine Inc., Susan discusses the tour of Powder Metal Inc. with Brad and Amy. They have obtained the following data:

Number of people observed working on the product per shift: 9 (Did you count the same?)

Materials used:	Powder metal at $25/lb
	Solvent at $2/lb
Materials used per bushing:	2 lb each
Total major investment:	Oven $750,000
	Press $750,000
Quality control instrumentation:	$250,000
Total investment:	$1,750,000 × 2 = $3,500,000
Maintenance as a percentage of investment:	2% (versus the standard 6%)

With this data, Susan modifies the utility and maintenance factors and the investment multiplier and uses the cost-estimating table to make the calculation shown in Figure 4-2. After adding profit, she obtains the potential selling price of the powder metal bushing.

Susan now has a whole new perspective on powder metal bushing costs. Her calculations prove that the powder metal material is by far the most important cost element in the final product. Mike had mentioned that they can't get a discount on this material because they don't order large quantities. Also, the process yield is a concern that Powder Metal is aware of and is working on.

Susan makes a quick calculation to see what effect it would have on the final price to Engine Inc. if they can assist Powder Metal Inc. with a couple of things. If they can help to get the price for the powder metal reduced to $20 per pound, and if their engineering department can help Powder Metal Inc. to maximize the efficiency of the process so that yields rise from 84 percent to 95 percent, she is sure it will make a huge difference in their cost. The following calculations show the impact Susan can have on the final price to her company if she is successful in negotiating a partnership program with Powder Metal Inc. under which they increase yields and lower material costs.

First, compare material costs under the current price of powder metal versus the reduced price Susan wants to obtain:

FIGURE 4-2.
Cost estimate for Powder Metal Inc.

EQUATION	ACTUAL DATA	ANSWER
TOTAL MATERIALS USED		
P x (U/y) [Price per unit quantity times (# ordered times weight divided by yield)]	Powder Metal: $25/lb x (50,000 x 2/.84) = Solvent: $2/lb x (50,000 x 2/84) =	$2,976,100 $ 238,095
UTILITIES		
TI x .01 [Total investment times 1%]	$3,500,000 x .01 =	$ 35,000
LABOR		
# x $ x 4800 [Number of operators times hourly rate times 4800]	10 x $20/hr x 4800 =	$ 960,000
MAINTENANCE		
TI x .02 [Total investment times 2%]	$3,500,000 x .02 =	$ 70,000
OVERHEADS		
L x .75 [Labor times 75%]	$960,000 x .75 =	$ 720,000
DEPRECIATION, TAXES, & INSURANCE		
TI x .11 [Total Investment times 11%]	$3,500,000 x .11 =	$ 385,000
Subtotal #1		$ 5,384,285
GENERAL & ADMINISTRATIVE		
Subtotal #1 x .15	$5,384,285 x .15 =	$ 807,643
Subtotal #2		$ 6,191,928
PROFIT		
Subtotal #2 x .18 [Subtotal #2 times 18%]	$6,191,928 x .18 =	$1,114,546
Final Price		$7,306,474
Selling Price/Item [Final price divided by the number to be manufactured]	$7,306,474/50,000 =	$150/ bushing

Current: $25 × (100,000/.84) = $2,976,190
New: $20 × (100,000/.95) = $2,105,263

Already, Susan sees a 30 percent decrease in material costs. This reduction will carry through the subtotals and profit margin, thereby reducing the final price considerably, as seen in Figure 4-3.

The difference is $28 per bushing, $122 versus the quoted price of $150. This reduction improves Engine Inc.'s bottom line by over a million dollars! And it all started with a plant tour and a calculation of estimated supplier costs!

It may seem that we've spent an inordinate amount of time preparing for step 1 of the Strategic Costing Process, but consider this. When you started elementary school, you learned such simple concepts as 1 + 1 = 2. You then advanced to more complicated equations that included subtraction, multiplication, and division. When you reached high school you were ready for algebra, geometry, and trigonometry. You had to advance a step at a time, which is what we're doing in this book. In school, if you didn't learn the simple concepts well enough to do them with ease, it was very hard to grasp more advanced mathematical functions.

In the same vein, you need to be so well versed in these first calculations that when we reach the second, third, and fourth steps in the process, you have no problems with the equations required. As a matter of fact, I encourage you to select some products or services that you are familiar with and do with them just what we've done in the last two chapters. You may be happily surprised at just how adept you have become at costing!

FIGURE 4-3.
Alternative cost estimate for Powder Metal Inc.

EQUATION	ACTUAL DATA	ANSWER
TOTAL MATERIALS USED		
P x (U/y) [Price per unit quantity times (# ordered times weight divided by yield)]	Powder Metal: $20/lb x (50,000 x 2/.95) = Solvent: $2/lb x (50,000 x 2/.95) =	$2,105,263 $ 210,526
UTILITIES		
TI x .01 [Total investment times 1%]	$3,500,000 x .01 =	$ 35,000
LABOR		
# x $ x 4800 [Number of operators times hourly rate times 4800]	10 x $20/hr x 4800 =	$ 960,000
MAINTENANCE		
TI x .02 [Total investment times 2%]	$3,500,000 x .02 =	$ 70,000
OVERHEADS		
L x .75 [Labor times 75%]	$960,000 x .75 =	$ 720,000
DEPRECIATION, TAXES, & INSURANCE		
TI x .11 [Total Investment times 11%]	$3,500,000 x .11 –	$ 385,000
Subtotal #1		$ 4,485,789
GENERAL & ADMINISTRATIVE		
Subtotal #1 x .15	$4,485,789 x .15 =	$ 672,868
Subtotal #2		$ 5,158,657
PROFIT		
Subtotal #2 x .18 [Subtotal #2 times 18%]	$5,158,657 x .18 =	$ 928,558
Final Price		$6,087,215
Selling Price/Item [Final price divided by the number to be manufactured]	$6,087,215/50,000 =	$122/ bushing

CHAPTER

5

NEGOTIATING WITH POWER

By estimating supplier costs and knowing where the major cost areas are you can plan for a negotiation that will lead to a better price. How? By joining with your supplier to reduce the largest area of cost, thereby reducing material costs to your company and improving your bottom line.

Remembering four tips will help you to maximize your effectiveness and ensure a satisfactory negotiation:

1. Always try for a win-win situation.
2. Leave yourself room to negotiate and compromise.
3. Be prepared.
4. Use your power. (Your power comes from the knowledge you bring to the table, your efforts, and your negotiating skills.)

Always Try for a Win-Win Situation

Achieving a win-win situation means obtaining from the negotiation the best outcome possible for both parties. If you are trying to build a long-term relationship with a supplier, you don't want to negotiate to the point at which the supplier is losing money. At the same time, you don't want to compromise your position too much. A negotiating strategy in which you try for the lowest possible price from your supplier might work the first time, but what is going to happen the next time you negotiate with these people? What goes around usually comes around, so if you negotiate a very good deal for your company the first time, the next time the other side will probably try to make up what they lost on the first deal! This cycle will continue until one of you decides it's not worth doing business with the other.

A win-win negotiation is not easy to accomplish most of the time. One side always has a little advantage due to all the complexities of a negotiation. It is possible for both parties to gain, but more often than not, one party wins more than the other. This chapter, I hope, gives you the resources to strive for a win-win negotiation, and, failing that, at least makes it possible for your company to win more times than it loses.

Leave Yourself Room to Negotiate and Compromise

Before entering the negotiation, determine the price you are going to try to obtain during the negotiation. This price should then be bracketed by two numbers that are acceptable to you, would still be profitable, and would improve your company's bottom line. If you are the buyer, the upper number is the highest price that you could accept and that would still improve the bottom line: the maximum acceptable price. Any price above that number is a deal buster. The lower number to establish is the price below which you would obtain an overadvantage in the negotiations and not a win-win situation: the minimum obtainable price. Figure 5-1 represents the three points from a buyer's perspective.

On the other hand, if you are the seller, the upper number to establish is the price above which you would obtain an overad-

FIGURE 5-1.
Buyer's perspective

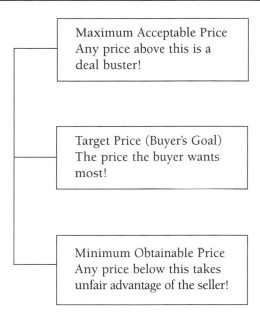

Maximum Acceptable Price
Any price above this is a
deal buster!

Target Price (Buyer's Goal)
The price the buyer wants
most!

Minimum Obtainable Price
Any price below this takes
unfair advantage of the seller!

vantage and not a win-win situation: the maximum obtainable price. The lower number from a seller's perspective is the lowest price you could accept and that would still improve your company's bottom line: the minimum acceptable price. Any price below that number is a deal buster. The seller's perspective is illustrated in Figure 5-2.

When you consider both the buyer's and the seller's perspectives, as in Figure 5-3, you'll notice an area of overlap. This is the area of win-win negotiation. In this area both sides have probably compromised a little, but both feel they have made a good deal and negotiated effectively.

Suppose the item being negotiated is the price of a new car. The buyer sees a beautiful car on the lot with a sticker price of $35,500. There is no trade-in car in this deal, so this is the maximum obtainable price of the car dealer (seller). The seller's minimum acceptable price is probably about $100 above cost—for this example, $28,500. This price still allows the seller to make a

FIGURE 5-2.
Seller's perspective

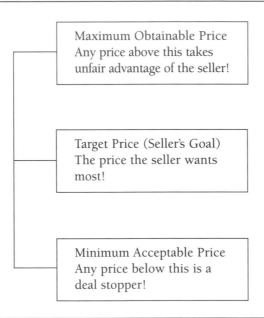

Maximum Obtainable Price
Any price above this takes
unfair advantage of the seller!

Target Price (Seller's Goal)
The price the seller wants
most!

Minimum Acceptable Price
Any price below this is a
deal stopper!

profit and improve the bottom line (especially if it's close to the
end of the month and inventory is high). The target price, therefore, is probably somewhere between; let's say $33,000. In our
bracketed form, the seller's perspective looks like Figure 5-4.

The knowledgeable buyer sees the sticker price of $35,500
and is, of course, unwilling to pay it, so the buyer's maximum
acceptable price is about $34,000, say. However, the buyer really
wants a percentage off the sticker price, so the target price is
$31,000. The best deal the buyer expects is to get the car at
dealer's cost. Without knowing what that cost is in reality, we
project it to be $28,000. (Books such as *Edmund's* give you the
sticker price and dealer's cost.) Figure 5-5 shows the buyer's perspective on this deal.

For this particular negotiation the maximum and minimum
prices for both the buyer and the seller have a wide area of overlap (from $28,500 to $34,000), and the negotiation will probably
result in a deal acceptable to both.

FIGURE 5-3.
Area of win-win negotiation

Buyer's Perspective   Seller's Perspective

FIGURE 5-4.
Auto dealer's perspective

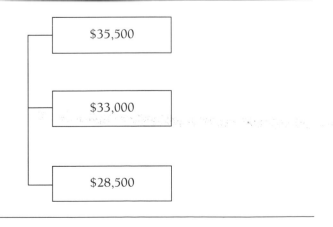

FIGURE 5-5.
Auto buyer's perspective

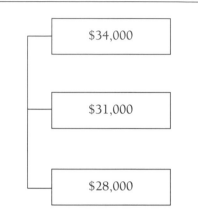

If you leave room to negotiate and compromise, your negotiation will have better chances of success.

Be Prepared

"Be prepared" is the old Boy Scout motto, and it has a lot of application to negotiations. Being prepared for a negotiation means doing your homework. It means reviewing estimated supplier costs, setting target prices of your own, along with maximum acceptable and minimum obtainable brackets, and choosing a strategy for negotiations. Ask yourself: What are the key areas on which to focus the discussion?

Use Your Power

Three areas of power can be used in a negotiation: knowledge, effort, and skill. The following case study illustrates just how much power you have when you follow the guidelines in this book before entering into negotiations.

Case Study: Negotiations With B&B Molders

Mike S. is a senior buyer for Calico Toys. Calico's hottest item this year is the X-men action figures. Calico expects to sell 7 million figures next year at a retail price of $10 each. Mike buys one of the major components of this toy, an injection-molded gizmo. He has been buying the gizmo from B&B Molders for the last two years. Mike has received three quotes to date; they are shown in Figure 5-6.

Mike would like to continue to do business with B&B Molders because it makes good quality parts, it has always shipped on time, and he has a good relationship with its sales force. In preparation for a negotiation that will take place later that month, he decides to visit the B&B facility and estimate the cost to produce the gizmo.

Mike assembles a team of four people for the visit to B&B Molders. The team collects the following data during their visit:

- One injection-molding machine is dedicated to making gizmos and can produce up to 8.5 million parts per year on a one-shift basis.
- Each machine has about 90 percent yield.
- Each machine has two operators, one inspector and one packer.
- Pay scale for the region is about $15 per hour base pay.
- Engineering confirms an injection-molding press would be about $250,000 new.
- Industry average profit margin for injection-molded parts is about 20 percent before tax.
- Manufacturing assures Mike that reject-grade plastic may be used for this part and is currently valued at $.60 per pound.
- There is one pound of plastic per gizmo.
- Price-volume history with B&B Molders for the gizmo is shown in Figure 5-7.

FIGURE 5-6.
Quote data for gizmo

Supplier	Price per Gizmo ($)	Total Dollars per Lot of 7 Million
B&B Molders	1.25	8.75 million
Morgan Plastics	1.10	7.70 million
Jones Brothers Inc.	1.35	9.45 million

FIGURE 5-7.
Price-volume data

	Volume Ordered (million)	Price per Gizmo ($)
2 years ago	2	1.50
1 year ago	3	1.28
Current quote	7	1.25

With all this information in hand, Mike now spends some time preparing for his meeting with B&B Molders.

Before reviewing Mike's calculations, put yourself in Mike's shoes. With the data presented, do your own calculations using Figure 5-8[1] and plan your strategy in preparation for the meeting. When you have finished, examine Mike's calculations in Figure 5-9. Did Mike do a good job as senior buyer of Calico Toys?

---

1. Also use the cost-estimating spreadsheet to estimate B&B Molders' costs.

FIGURE 5-8.
Cost-estimating table

TOTAL MATERIALS USED		
P x (U/y) [Price per unit quantity times (# ordered times weight divided by yield)]		
UTILITIES		
TI x .02 [Total investment times 2%]		
LABOR		
# x $ x 4800 [Number of operators times hourly rate times 4800]		
MAINTENANCE		
TI x .06 [Total investment times 6%]		
OVERHEADS		
L x .75 [Labor times 75%]		
DEPRECIATION, TAXES, & INSURANCE		
TI x .11 [Total Investment times 11%]		
Subtotal #1		
GENERAL & ADMINISTRATIVE		
Subtotal #1 x .15		
Subtotal #2		
PROFIT		
Subtotal #2 x PM [Subtotal #2 times % estimated profit margin]		
Final Price		
Selling Price/Item [Final price divided by the number to be manufactured]		

FIGURE 5-9.
Cost estimate for B&B Molders

PROJECTED TOTAL COSTS, of

B&B Molders

COS, © 1989, Dale Brethauer

BASIC PREMISES:

Number of Operators:	4
Hourly Wage Rate:	$15.00
Material Price:	$0.60
Process Yield:	90%
Sales Volume:	7,000,000
Total Investment:	$750,000

	$/YEAR	$/PIECE
VARIABLE COST		
Materials	$4,666,667	$0.67
Utilities	$15,000	$0.00
Subtotal Variable Costs	$4,681,667	$0.67
FIXED COSTS		
Labor	$287,958	$0.04
Equipment Maintenance	$45,000	$0.01
Overhead	$215,969	$0.03
Property Taxes and Insurance	$7,500	$0.00
Equipment Allocations	$75,000	$0.01
Subtotal Fixed Costs	$631,427	$0.09
SUBTOTAL VARIABLE AND FIXED COSTS	$5,313,093	$0.76
GENERAL AND ADMINISTRATIVE COSTS		
Selling Expense	$265,655	$0.04
Administration	$265,655	$0.04
Distribution	$265,655	$0.04
TOTAL COSTS	$6,110,057	$0.87

6

HOW TO ESTIMATE
ALMOST ANYTHING

Now that you've gotten your feet wet in the beginning stages of the Strategic Costing Process, you need a little practice to become proficient as you begin to understand the costing concepts.

This chapter discusses three practical application of the equations detailed in Chapter 3. Estimates for two common products and one common service are made. The products are a pepperoni pizza and a wooden pallet; the service is the dry cleaning of a shirt.

Pepperoni Pizza

First, let's estimate the cost of a pepperoni pizza from Ma and Pa's Pizzeria. Figure 6-1 gives the cost of materials.

FIGURE 6-1.
Calculation of material cost for Ma and Pa's Pizzeria

Ingredients	Amount (lb)	Price per Pound	Subtotal ($)
Dough	2	0.50	1.00
Tomato sauce	0.5	0.50	0.25
Cheese	1	1.00	1.00
Pepperoni	0.5	2.00	0.50
Total			2.75/pizza

Operators

For Ma and Pa's Pizzeria, usually only one operator runs the pizza oven. This operator, if not the owner, will be paid slightly over minimum wage—let's say $10.00 per hour.

Sales Volume

For this shop the busiest times of the day are the lunch and dinner hours. Assume that during each of those hours they produce 20 pizzas. That is 40, plus another 25 pizzas for the remainder of the day, for a total of 65 pizzas per day. Assuming the shop is open 6 days a week, 52 weeks a year, yearly production is:

$$\text{65 pizzas/day} \times \text{6 days/week} \times \text{52 weeks/year}$$
$$= \text{20,380 pizzas/year}$$

Total Investment

The biggest investment is the oven, at approximately $50,000, and an additional $25,000 of equipment. The surrounding building, counter, and so forth, take the total shop investment to $150,000.

Use these data, and enter them into the cost-estimating table (Figure 6-2) to estimate the costs. What total cost do you get for a pepperoni pizza? Compare your numbers with our calculated sheet (Figure 6-3). Talk with your local pizza shop owner about the validity of these costs.

FIGURE 6-2.

Cost-estimating table

TOTAL MATERIALS USED		
P x (U/y) [Price per unit quantity times (# ordered times weight divided by yield)]		
UTILITIES		
TI x .02 [Total investment times 2%]		
LABOR		
# x $ x 4800 [Number of operators times hourly rate times 4800]		
MAINTENANCE		
TI x .06 [Total investment times 6%]		
OVERHEADS		
L x .75 [Labor times 75%]		
DEPRECIATION, TAXES, & INSURANCE		
TI x .11 [Total Investment times 11%]		
Subtotal #1		
GENERAL & ADMINISTRATIVE		
Subtotal #1 x .15		
Subtotal #2		
PROFIT		
Subtotal #2 x PM [Subtotal #2 times % estimated profit margin]		
Final Price		
Selling Price/Item [Final price divided by the number to be manufactured]		

FIGURE 6-3.

Cost estimate for Ma and Pa's Pizzeria

PROJECTED TOTAL COSTS, of

Ma and Pa's Pizzeria

COS, © 1989, Dale Brethauer

BASIC PREMISES:

Number of Operators:	1
Hourly Wage Rate:	$10.00
Material Price:	$2.75
Process Yield:	100%
Sales Volume:	20,000
Total Investment:	$150,000

	$/YEAR	$/PIECE
VARIABLE COST		
Materials	$55,000	$2.75
Utilities	$3,000	$0.15
Subtotal Variable Costs	$58,000	$2.90
FIXED COSTS		
Labor	$47,993	$2.40
Equipment Maintenance	$9,000	$0.45
Overhead	$35,995	$1.80
Property Taxes and Insurance	$1,500	$0.08
Equipment Allocations	$15,000	$0.75
Subtotal Fixed Costs	$109,488	$5.47
SUBTOTAL VARIABLE AND FIXED COSTS	$167,488	$8.37
GENERAL AND ADMINISTRATIVE COSTS		
Selling Expense	$8,374	$0.42
Administration	$8,374	$0.42
Distribution	$8,374	$0.42
TOTAL COSTS	$192,611	$9.63

Wooden Pallets

About six months after taking one of my seminars, a senior buyer called me and said, "Okay, I have just gotten a quote for 100,000 wooden pallets for delivery next year. I have visited the vendor's facility and have calculated a cost for wooden pallets. I just want to check my calculations. Can I give you the necessary numbers to check my numbers?" I said, "Sure!" I always enjoy reconnecting with people I've worked with to advance their understanding of business economics.

He gave me the following data:

- Three operators work together to assemble and stack pallets, one handling materials and the other two assembling pallets.
- The local base pay scale for unskilled labor is only $12.50 per hour.
- The main material for the pallets is 4-inch-wide No. 2 pine boards at $.10 per board-foot, plus support blocks at the ends.
- Pallets are 4 feet by 4 feet.
- There are approximately 70 board-feet per pallet.
- A crew of three operators can produce 100,000 pallets per shift.
- They work in a butler-style building with very little automation, a couple of jigs and fixtures, two auto hammers, and a forklift.

Figure the costs for the wooden pallets using the cost-estimating table (Figure 6-4). My cost-estimating worksheet is shown in Figure 6-5.

What was very satisfying was that my figures matched exactly what the former student had calculated and he said, "I now feel confident in ordering 100,000 pallets from this vendor."

FIGURE 6-4.
Cost estimating table

TOTAL MATERIALS USED		
P x (U/y) [Price per unit quantity times (# ordered times weight divided by yield)]		
UTILITIES		
TI x .02 [Total investment times 2%]		
LABOR		
# x $ x 4800 [Number of operators times hourly rate times 4800]		
MAINTENANCE		
TI x .06 [Total investment times 6%]		
OVERHEADS		
L x .75 [Labor times 75%]		
DEPRECIATION, TAXES, & INSURANCE		
TI x .11 [Total Investment times 11%]		
Subtotal #1		
GENERAL & ADMINISTRATIVE		
Subtotal #1 x .15		
Subtotal #2		
PROFIT		
Subtotal #2 x PM [Subtotal #2 times % estimated profit margin]		
Final Price		
Selling Price/Item [Final price divided by the number to be manufactured]		

FIGURE 6-5.
Cost estimate for wooden pallets

PROJECTED TOTAL COSTS, of

Wooden Pallets

COS, © 1989, Dale Brethauer

BASIC PREMISES:

Number of Operators:	3
Hourly Wage Rate:	$12.50
Material Price:	$7.10
Process Yield:	100%
Sales Volume:	100,000
Total Investment:	$10,000

	$/YEAR	$/PIECE
VARIABLE COST		
Materials	$710,000	$7.10
Utilities	$200	$0.00
Subtotal Variable Costs	$710,200	$7.10
FIXED COSTS		
Labor	$179,974	$1.80
Equipment Maintenance	$600	$0.01
Overhead	$134,980	$1.35
Property Taxes and Insurance	$100	$0.00
Equipment Allocations	$1,000	$0.01
Subtotal Fixed Costs	$316,654	$3.17
SUBTOTAL VARIABLE AND FIXED COSTS	$1,026,854	$10.27
GENERAL AND ADMINISTRATIVE COSTS		
Selling Expense	$51,343	$0.51
Administration	$51,343	$0.51
Distribution	$51,343	$0.51
TOTAL COSTS	$1,180,882	$11.81

The quote he had received from the vendor was for $13 per pallet. This price seemed very reasonable, giving the vendor about 10 percent pretax profit, and therefore the senior buyer went ahead with a purchase order for $1.3 million worth of new pallets.

Dry Cleaning of a Dress Shirt

To collect the data to estimate the total costs of dry cleaning a dress shirt, I visited my local dry cleaner and asked the following questions (I am a friend of the owners, so they were pretty open about supplying the requested information):

- Approximately how many dress shirts do you dry clean in an hour? In a year?
- How many people operate the steam presses?
- How many presses and dry clean machines do you have?
- About how much do they cost?

I already knew the price per shirt from my most recent ticket. Six shirts cost $8.10, or $1.35 per shirt.

From the answers I received from my dry cleaner I was able to formulate the following projections to make a cost estimate for the service of dry cleaning a dress shirt. This may be seen on the cost estimate in Figure 6-6.

Using these data, I plugged all the numbers into the cost-estimating model and came up with a total cost of $1.18. The calculation was based on one operator steam pressing 45 shirts per hour:

$$45 \text{ shirts/hour} \times 2,080 \text{ hours/year} = 93,600 \text{ shirts/year}$$

For two steam press operators you would, of course, double that amount to 190,000 shirts per year. With a price of $1.35 per shirt and a cost of $1.18 that gives $.17 for profit, or 13 percent pre-tax profit.

It is interesting to note that for this service the volume that an operator can produce is critical to reaching this cost and achieving a profitable business. If the operators only produce 40 shirts per hour, total yearly production for two operators is about 165,000 shirts per year. If we substituted this number for the 190,000 shirts per year in our original calculation, total cost is $1.35 (see Figure 6-7).

This new calculation shows no profit. This reveals to the dry cleaner owner how critical the production of the press operator is in making sure the dry cleaner is profitable! It also shows you how valuable the calculations are, not only in maintaining a profitable business, but also in growing a bigger business with more profits.

You are now ready to begin strategic costing because you have mastered all the necessary tools. We have our puzzle outline, so let's start to put the pieces into place.

FIGURE 6-6.
Cost estimate for dry cleaning a dress shirt

PROJECTED TOTAL COSTS, of

Dress Shirts

COS, © 1989, Dale Brethauer

BASIC PREMISES:

Number of Operators:	3
Hourly Wage Rate:	$7.00
Material Price:	$0.05
Process Yield:	100%
Sales Volume:	190,000
Total Investment:	$50,000

	$/YEAR	$/PIECE
VARIABLE COST		
Materials	$9,500	$0.05
Utilities	$1,000	$0.01
Subtotal Variable Costs	$10,500	$0.06
FIXED COSTS		
Labor	$100,785	$0.53
Equipment Maintenance	$3,000	$0.02
Overhead	$75,589	$0.40
Property Taxes and Insurance	$500	$0.00
Equipment Allocations	$5,000	$0.01
Subtotal Fixed Costs	$184,874	$0.97
SUBTOTAL VARIABLE AND FIXED COSTS	$195,374	$1.03
GENERAL AND ADMINISTRATIVE COSTS		
Selling Expense	$9,769	$0.05
Administration	$9,769	$0.05
Distribution	$9,769	$0.05
TOTAL COSTS	$224,681	$1.18

FIGURE 6-7.
Alternative cost estimate for dry cleaning a dress shirt

PROJECTED TOTAL COSTS, of

Dress Shirts–Alternate

COS, © 1989, Dale Brethauer

BASIC PREMISES:

Number of Operators:	3
Hourly Wage Rate:	$7.00
Material Price:	$0.05
Process Yield:	100%
Sales Volume:	165,000
Total Investment:	$50,000

	$/YEAR	$/PIECE
VARIABLE COST		
Materials	$8,250	$0.05
Utilities	$1,000	$0.01
Subtotal Variable Costs	$9,250	$0.06
FIXED COSTS		
Labor	$100,785	$0.61
Equipment Maintenance	$3,000	$0.02
Overhead	$75,589	$0.46
Property Taxes and Insurance	$500	$0.00
Equipment Allocations	$5,000	$0.03
Subtotal Fixed Costs	$184,874	$1.12
SUBTOTAL VARIABLE AND FIXED COSTS	$194,124	$1.18
GENERAL AND ADMINISTRATIVE COSTS		
Selling Expense	$9,706	$0.06
Administration	$9,706	$0.06
Distribution	$9,706	$0.06
TOTAL COSTS	$223,243	$1.35

STEP 2:
ESTIMATE COMPETITOR COSTS

CHAPTER

COMPETITIVE

ASSESSMENT

Keeping up with the competition does not have to be a shot in the dark, or as unreliable as having your fortune told. Competitive assessment provides the information needed to enable a company to take the initiative in the marketplace. This proactive posture keeps a company at the forefront of its industrial sector and ultimately keeps it profitable and in business. Through competitive assessment, your company can also determine how competitive the competition is now, if they will be a threat should they improve their productivity, and what their cost of doing business is. Your company might choose to do a competitive assessment study if:

- Your competition has announced a product line or service expansion.
- Your competition has announced that it is entering a market where your company is a key player.
- Your company has noticed that your market share is decreasing or you plan to expand your own facilities.

Competitive assessment means more than benchmarking others in your industrial sector. Competitive assessment means a thorough study of your competitors' business, investments, costs, cash flow, and financial position, and a projection of their strengths and weaknesses. This information may be difficult to gather, but it allows you to make solid business decisions that keep your company competitive and the "best of the best."

Many companies benchmark. Benchmarking occurs when companies in the same industry sit down together and openly discuss such topics as current wage rates, union involvement, employee benefits, R&D as a percentage of sales, and so forth. These nonthreatening metrics are shared freely.

Another area of competitive analysis is evaluation of the marketplace. Here, again, the information is in the public domain and merely needs to be gathered in a systematic manner. It may be published in trade journals or tracked by common customer contacts. Items used to track the marketplace are things like shipments, current prices, and the like.

Benchmarks and marketplace information are the starting points for any competitive assessment, but a good study must go further. Information now becomes more difficult to obtain. To make a good competitive assessment, a company needs to estimate its competitors' processes, investments associated with the processes, costs associated with the processes, and cash flow and to project their probable future business strategies.

This is not a trivial task, and it might seem impossible; but if approached methodically, utilizing economic models that I discuss in this book, the task is doable. And the rewards of a solid competitive assessment can make a great difference in your company's profitability.

The Society of Competitive Intelligence Professionals states that "using ethical and legal research techniques, your company can obtain an average of 90% or more of your intelligence needs, enough to make critical business decisions."

Competitive assessment helps management set strategic objectives and goals and design strategic programs and plans for:

- New product introduction
- New businesses and new ventures
- R&D decisions

- Mergers and acquisitions
- Capacity expansions

Competitor Costs

In Step 1, we looked at a model for calculating the total costs of a product or service. This model was then used to estimate supplier costs. Before estimating these costs, however, it was necessary to gather data on the key cost drivers: materials used, labor, and total investment. One of the best ways to gather these data is by taking plant tours of supplier facilities and asking intelligent questions to better understand both the production process itself and the investment, materials, and labor used in the process. Once that information was obtained, it was possible to use the cost-estimating model. Getting information on a supplier's production process is much easier than getting the required data for a competitor because you can't walk through the competitor's plant and ask questions. However, three alternative methods can get you the data needed to estimate competitor costs:

1. Search existing patents.
2. Make legal investigations.
3. Search open literature—newspapers and trade journals.

Search Existing Patents

Patents contain a wealth of information. Indeed, patents are two-edged swords. The more a company values its technology, the more details it wants to claim in a patent in order to protect its intellectual property. But the more the company claims, the more it teaches you about its process. If your competitors value their process technology, you can usually learn how they make their products—all the essential materials used and the recipes, or percentages, according to which they are combined. Remember, what you are trying to learn about each competitor is materials used, total investment, and labor. From patents you can usually learn two of the major pieces of data: materials used and processes to manufacture the product. With information from a patent, and with an understanding of the production process, your company's engineering staff can put together a process flow diagram and an investment estimate on a replacement basis for the equipment needed to make the product.

Consider the patent from the Patent Bureau of Japan in the appendix of this chapter. This application, entitled "A Method of Manufacturing a Polyurethane Elastic Body," illustrates what information may be extracted from a typical patent. Note that section 3 of the patent, "Detailed Description of the Invention," describes the entire production process in the second paragraph. It also describes the essential materials used.

The patent states that a diol compound is mixed with diisocyanate in the first reactor. This mixture (known as a prepolymer) is then blended with an inactive polar organic solvent in a dissolver. This mixture is then blended with a diamine compound in the second reactor. The resulting polymer then goes to spinning. In this paragraph the Toyobo Company divulges the process by which it produces the polymer to manufacture elastic bodies, and from this information we can extract a list of the equipment and essential materials needed:

Equipment List
- Two reactors
- One dissolver

Essential Materials List
- Diol compound
- Diisocyanate
- Polar organic solvent
- Diamine compound

Patent information abstracts or complete copies of filings may be obtained at the U.S. Patent Office in Washington, D.C. You need to know one of the following pieces of information to make a search: inventor's name, corporate assignation, title, or product name. Patents can be cleared by:

Commissioner of Patents
Patent and Trademark Office
Box 9
Washington, D.C. 20231

Another source of searchable patent information is the Internet. IBM Corporation has made most U.S. patents available to the general public. The IBM patent server is found at http://www.ibm.com/patents. Once you are at this web site the search for a particular patent can be done very easily by using IBM's menu-driven features.

Make Legal Investigations

Many consultants specialize in legal investigations of companies in various business sectors. They search patents, read open literature, and make personal contacts with former employees, customers, and equipment suppliers.

The best criterion for choosing a consultant is someone's personal experience. If you have not worked with a consultant before, ask around. The primary form of marketing for consultants is word of mouth. Ask within your company whether anyone has used a consultant to help gather competitive intelligence. If not, a number of resources and publications list consultants— for example:

- *Bradford's Directory of Marketing Research Agencies and Management Consultants in the United States and the World* (Bradford's, Middleburg, Virginia)
- *Consultants and Consulting Organizations Directory* (Gale Research, Detroit, Michigan)
- *Who's Who in Consulting* (Gale Research, Detroit, Michigan)
- *Directory of Management Consultants* (Consultants News, Fitzwilliam, New Hampshire)
- *Directory of Members* (Institute of Management Consultants, New York)

- *Directory of Member Firms* (New York Association of Consulting Management Engineers)
- *Directory of Research Sales* (Marketing Research Associates)

It is important to establish goals for a competitive assessment study, prepare a signed agreement, and develop a project time line before turning a consultant loose. A consultant can also help to check data you have already gathered, so be specific when setting goals and detailing the information you require.

For example, earlier we looked at a patent that described a process to manufacture elastic bodies. It is similar to the process shown in Figure 7-1. You may want to ask a consultant to research this process and determine when it was first brought onstream.

Gathering competitive assessment data is rather like solving a crossword puzzle. You probably won't be 100 percent sure about any single datum you gather. However, enough data coming from various sources helps to confirm or reject that piece of information. The solver of a crossword puzzle might enter an answer to a down clue without being 100 percent sure it's correct. But when the solver enters an across answer that confirms a letter of the previously entered down answer, he or she gains confidence in the earlier entry. This analogy illustrates exactly how gathering and confirming competitive data works. The more independent sources confirm your data, the more sure you are that your data are good and can be used with confidence to estimate competitor costs.

Imagine you ask an independent competitive assessment consultant to identify the method of manufacturing elastic bodies and then receive the following process description: "Four essential materials are mixed together in a three-step process: two reaction steps and one dissolving step. The reactors need to be heated, jacketed, and under constant agitation. The dissolver is rather sophisticated and only manufactured by two vendors: PDQ Machinery and Dissolve Inc." Knowing what you do about the Toyobo patent you would probably feel good about that information and feel confident

FIGURE 7-1.

Polymer process

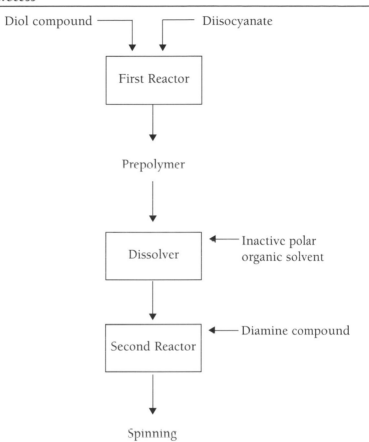

proceeding to develop an equipment list and then a total investment number, one of the three pieces of data you need to estimate costs.

Search Open Literature

Market segment overviews, company financials, management profiles, and company histories can be obtained through open literature. You can gain a perspective on a market by searching trade magazines, especially their annual issues, which usually give data on major plants, sales, and markets. From U.S. Department of Commerce publications you can obtain industry shipments and trends. Private publishing and market research firms also issue market studies.

Consumer databases can answer such questions as:

- What articles are written on this market?
- Which companies are associated with this product group?
- Are there available patents?
- What are the major magazines for this industry?
- Who are the leading experts in the industry?

The top five databases are:

Bibliographic Retrieval Service
1200 Route 7
Latham, NY 12110
518/783-1161

Dialog
3460 Hillview Avenue
Palo Alto, CA 94304
415/858-3785

Nexis
Mead Data Central
PO Box 933
Dayton, OH 45401
513/859-1611

SDC/Orbit
Systems Development Corporation
2500 Colorado Avenue
Santa Monica, CA 90406
213/820-4111

Dow Jones/News Retrieval
PO Box 300
Princeton, NJ 08540

Local newspapers can also give you a wealth of information about the competitors. When you begin a competitive assessment one of the first things to consider is hiring a local "clipping service" in the competitor's geographic region. This service will clip all local newspaper articles that mention the competitor being studied. Companies are always interested in community relations and want to be good neighbors. They proudly publish in local newspapers such things as how many people from the community they employ at a certain facility, how much they have invested in their facilities, and even sometimes future plans that will affect the regions surrounding their facilities.

Let's say, for example, you are doing a competitive assessment of a company and have hired a clipping service in the company's area. (You know it is building a plant near a major city.) One day the clipping service sends you an article that says, "Next week Company X will be bringing their process equipment into their new facility." Well, guess where you need to be next week? That's right, next to that facility, taking notes on the equipment being shipped in, all legal and ethical. Just from reading an article in the local newspaper you can be present when a competitor's major equipment is installed. From this exposure you can then put together an equipment list with confidence.

It can also be very enlightening to drive by your competitor's facility. You might be able to answer questions like:

- How well do they maintain their assets?
- How many cars are in the parking lot?
- How many shifts do they work?
- Do they generate their own power?
- Are they located close to rail or water transportation?

Once you feel confident about your data you can use the cost-estimating model to calculate your competitor's product or service costs.

Case Study: Competitive Assessment of Baraq Company versus Mother Board Inc.

Baraq Company manufactures computer board components and assembles the final board. Four major companies worldwide manufacture and assemble computer boards, and Baraq currently has 40 percent of the market share. Mother Board, one of its competitors, estimates that it can enter the $200 million market because of a potentially proprietary new circuit design and state-of-the-art automation assembly process that gives it the ability to turn out boards at a total cost of $32.97 each. Mother Board's management believes that if the company's projected cost is 25 percent lower than Baraq's, this cost advantage added to the proprietary technology will allow Mother Board to be a major player in this market.

Mother Board must determine whether it wants to enter this market. Bill leads a team of four people from R&D, manufacturing, purchasing, and engineering through a review of the following plan, which will allow them to assess Baraq's capabilities and costs:

1. Do a patent search to study Baraq's technology.
2. Hire a consultant to study the market value of Baraq's technology.
3. Study Baraq's expansion philosophy from open literature and local newspapers. (Baraq's headquarters and main plant are located in Palo Alto, California.)

In addition, Bill develops a checklist of information needed to estimate Baraq's costs and possible information sources. He has recently read a dynamite book on the Strategic Costing Process and is eager to put what he's learned to use. He knows that if he can obtain good information on materials, operators, and total investment, he can use the cost-estimating model to calculate Baraq's costs. His checklist is shown in Figure 7-2.

Bill's team projects that they will need a budget of $100,000, and that the information will take approximately three months to

FIGURE 7-2.
Competitive information needed

Information Needed	Information Source	Associated Cost Driver
1. Technology	Patents	Investment
2. Assembly process	Patents	Investment
3. Essential materials	Disassembly engineer	Materials
4. Operations	Outside consultant	Labor

gather. Mother Board's potential market, as indicated by earlier estimates, could be $50 million annually. Management decides this is time and money well spent, so the analysis begins!

After conducting a patent search the team agrees that Baraq's technology appears sound. Darrin, the engineer on the team, lays out a possible process flow diagram and equipment list. He then contacts equipment vendors and estimates that the equipment used for board assembly at Baraq's Palo Alto plant has a $5 million replacement value. To account for installation of equipment, building, power, and general services and project management, he multiplies this number by three, taking it to a $15 million total investment. The consultant finds that the facility was built four years ago. However, to use the cost-estimating model, Darrin knows he needs investment in today's replacement dollars. He reports his findings to Bill.

Meanwhile, the team has ordered Baraq's product, taken it apart, and determined an essential materials cost of $31.00 per board.

The last part of the puzzle is to estimate how many operators work to assemble the boards. Linda, a first-line supervisor at Mother Board's New Hampshire assembly plant, works with Darrin's process flow diagram and staffs the process with twenty-four people per shift. To manufacture Baraq's market volume would require them to work four shifts per day. Thus ninety-six people work full time to produce the 1.25 million special computer boards Baraq ships per year. A call to the Palo Alto Chamber of Commerce confirms the wage rate for the area at $15.00 per hour.

Bill now takes all this information and plugs it into the cost-estimating model to obtain the cost sheet shown in Figure 7-3.

FIGURE 7-3.

Cost estimate for Baraq Company

PROJECTED TOTAL COSTS, of

Baraq's Board Costs

COS, © 1989, Dale Brethauer

BASIC PREMISES:

Number of Operators:	96
Hourly Wage Rate:	$15.00
Material Price:	$31.00
Process Yield:	90%
Sales Volume:	1,250,000
Total Investment:	$15,000,000

	$/YEAR	$/PIECE
VARIABLE COST		
Materials	$43,055,555	$34.44
Utilities	$300,000	$0.24
Subtotal Variable Costs	$43,355,556	$34.68
FIXED COSTS		
Labor	$6,910,996	$5.53
Equipment Maintenance	$900,000	$0.72
Overhead	$5,183,247	$4.15
Property Taxes and Insurance	$150,000	$0.12
Equipment Allocations	$1,500,000	$1.20
Subtotal Fixed Costs	$14,644,242	$11.72
SUBTOTAL VARIABLE AND FIXED COSTS	$57,999,798	$46.40
GENERAL AND ADMINISTRATIVE COSTS		
Selling Expense	$2,899,990	$2.32
Administration	$2,899,990	$2.32
Distribution	$2,899,990	$2.32
TOTAL COSTS	$66,699,768	$53.36

The model predicts annual costs of $66,669,768, or $53.36 per board. This estimate corresponds well with Baraq's $75.00 per board selling price. A comparison of this cost with Mother Board's estimates for its own product shows almost a 40 percent lower cost for Mother Board. With these findings Mother Board is confident that it can profitably enter this market. However, before making a final decision, management asks Bill to work with Bev, of the finance department, on a financial analysis of Baraq. If Baraq is financially very strong, Mother Board might choose to be less aggressive toward Baraq's market, realizing Baraq has the financial strength to engage in a price war while improving its internal cost structure.

Competitor Financial Strength

What should you know about a competitor's financial position? You need to know its financial strengths and weaknesses. For a publicly traded company all necessary information may be ascertained from its annual report. If your competitor is a privately held company, financial information can usually be obtained from a Dun & Bradstreet report.

From a competitor's income statement, balance sheet, and cash flow statement, you can calculate ratios that indicate its financial strength. Also, you can compare its profit margins and uses of cash with those for your own company, as well as for others within your industrial sector. When planning strategies, you should know your competitor's financial strengths and past history of spending in order to anticipate its reactions.

Income Statement

The income statement shows profits, after taxes and expenses are subtracted from revenues earned. Other names for the income statement are the "P&L" (profit and loss) statement, the statement of earnings, and the statement of operations. The basic formula for the income statement is:

$$\text{Revenues} - \text{Expenses} = \text{Pretax income}$$
$$\text{Pretax income} - \text{Taxes} = \text{Net income}$$

An income statement typically starts with revenues. Net sales or operating revenues is what the competitor actually sold. The competitor's income statement shows its cost of goods sold. For a manufacturer, this is the cost to produce the product. For a service company, this is the cost to provide the service, which is usually associated labor. Next, the income statement shows general and administrative costs. These are expenses associated with the core business such as selling, administrative, R&D, and staff expenses. The last expense is depreciation. Subtracting these expenses from gross revenues yields pretax income. Income tax, usually about 40 percent for both federal and state, is then subtracted to obtain after-tax profit, or the bottom line. A typical income statement is shown in Figure 7-4.

Balance Sheet

A competitor's balance sheet shows assets such as cash, accounts receivable, inventory, and fixed assets (buildings and equipment) compared to liabilities and owner's equity. As the

FIGURE 7-4.
Income statement for Sample Inc.

Item	Transaction Amount (thousand $)	Balance (thousand $)
Revenues		5,000
– Cost of goods sold	3,000	
– General and administrative costs	1,000	
– Depreciation	500	
Subtotal of expenses	4,500	
Pretax income		500
Income taxes (40%)	200	
Net income		300

title implies, assets must equal or balance liabilities plus owner's equity. The basic equation is:

$$Assets = Liabilities + Equity$$

Equity is also called net worth. A sample balance sheet is shown in Figure 7-5.

Statement of Cash Flow

Both the income statement and the balance sheet are snapshots in time, usually the last day of the fiscal year. The statement of cash flow shows how a competitor used cash from operations during the year. This information is useful for understanding its decision-making philosophy about cash. After-tax income plus depreciation equals cash from operations. (Remember that depreciation must be added back to the cash stream because it is a noncash expense that the government allows to be subtracted from revenues; it is not subject to taxes. However, no money changes hands, so the depreciation amount must be added back into the cash flow stream.)

A company can do three things with cash from operations.

1. It may make changes in its working capital, such as increasing or decreasing its accounts receivable or accounts payable, or changing the levels of its inventory.

FIGURE 7-5.

Balance sheet for Sample Inc.

Assets (thousand $)		Liabilities (thousand $)	
Cash	500	Accounts payable	1,350
Accounts receivable	2,000	Short-term debt	250
Inventory	1,000		
Current assets	3,500	Current liabilities	1,600
Fixed assets		Long-term debt	3,000
(building and equipment)	8,000	Owner's equity	6,900
	11,500		11,500

2. It may reinvest in its business by acquiring or building new facilities (buildings, land, and equipment).
3. It may either increase or decrease its debt position.

A sample statement of cash flow is shown in Figure 7-6. (A full explanation of the cash flow statement is given in Chapter 9.)

Financial Ratios

Examining financial ratios is one of the most common ways of evaluating a competitor's strengths and weaknesses. Three of the best ratios to calculate for this evaluation are current ratio, debt-to-equity ratio, and the return-on-equity ratio. (These ratios can be calculated automatically by using the Financial Ratio Calculation spreadsheet on the disk. Enter information from the income statement and balance sheet, and the spreadsheet will calculate fifteen key performance ratios.)

FIGURE 7-6.
Statement of cash flow for Sample Inc.

Item (thousand $)		
Net income		500
Depreciation		800
		1,300
Decrease (increase) in accounts receivable	(300)	
Increase (decrease) in accounts payable	1,000	
Decrease (increase) in inventory	(500)	
Cash flow from operations	200	1,500
Purchase of fixed assets	(5,000)	
Cash flow from investing	(5,000)	(3,500)
Increase (decrease) in borrowing	4,000	
Dividends	(500)	
Cash flow from financing	3,500	0
Cash increase (decrease)		0

Current Ratio. The current ratio is a broad-based view of a competitor's overall liquidity. If it is a liquid company, it should be able to undertake product and capacity expansion plans. The current ratio is:

$$\frac{\text{Current assets}}{\text{Current liabilities}}$$

As a rule of thumb this ratio should be about 2:1. However, it's better to compare your competitor's ratio with the industry norm, by using a publication such as Dun & Bradstreet's "Industry Norms and Key Business Ratios." This is done by looking up your competitor's standard industrial classification (SIC) number and comparing its current ratio with the norm for that industrial sector. A sample page of Dun & Bradstreet's publication is reprinted in Figure 7-7 for the SIC 2851–2875.

Note that for SIC 2869 (no breakdown) the industry norm for the current ratio is 1.7. What is Sample Inc.'s current ratio? If it is in SIC 2869, how does it compare? Sample Inc.'s current ratio is:

$$\text{CA/CL} = 3,500/1,600 = 2.2$$

Sample Inc. is strong compared to others in its industrial sector, because a slightly higher current ratio is better.

Debt-to-Equity Ratio. The next important ratio is the debt-to-equity ratio. This ratio measures a competitor's financial obligations. A good ratio here also means it can pursue aggressive strategies. This ratio is calculated as:

$$\frac{\text{Total liabilities}}{\text{Owner's equity}}$$

Sample Inc.'s debt-to-equity ratio is:

$$\text{TL/OE} = 4,600/6,900 = 0.7, \text{ or } 70\%$$

FIGURE 7-7.

Dun & Bradstreet industry norms

RATIOS	SIC 2851 PAINTS, ALLIED PRDTS INDUSTRY ASSETS $5,000,000–$25,000,000 1997 (20 Establishments)			SIC 2851 PAINTS, ALLIED PRDTS INDUSTRY ASSETS OVER $50,000,000 1997 (14 Establishments)			SIC 2865 CYCL CRDS, INTRMDTES (NO BREAKDOWN) 1997 (27 Establishments)			SIC 2869 IND ORG CHEM, NEC (NO BREAKDOWN) 1997 (93 Establishments)		
	UQ	MED	LQ	UQ	MED	LQ	UQ	MED	LQ	UQ	MED	LQ
SOLVENCY												
Quick Ratio (times)	1.6	1.2	1.1	1.2	1.0	0.9	1.9	1.3	0.9	1.6	0.9	0.6
Current Ratio (times)	3.1	2.6	2.2	2.3	1.6	1.4	3.3	2.4	1.8	3.0	1.7	1.2
Curr Liab To Nw (%)	32.7	51.9	65.7	51.2	63.6	70.6	23.9	45.8	92.7	25.2	44.9	95.6
Curr Liab To Inv (%)	69.8	81.4	112.5	119.0	183.4	222.1	73.1	97.6	224.4	89.2	149.9	225.0
Total Liab To Nw (%)	50.7	77.8	140.8	91.7	130.8	184.3	28.1	64.7	192.4	39.1	89.1	169.3
Fixed Assets To Nw (%)	35.1	57.7	78.4	60.6	86.8	116.1	30.8	53.8	72.4	29.9	57.3	116.5
EFFICIENCY												
Coll Period (days)	28.8	38.3	53.7	63.9	77.2	80.3	41.0	46.6	57.5	34.5	47.8	60.8
Sales To Inv (times)	8.4	6.7	5.8	9.2	8.6	6.2	13.5	8.2	5.4	15.8	9.3	6.1
Assets To Sales (%)	39.4	45.9	56.3	61.1	86.0	103.1	35.5	51.4	86.8	44.8	74.2	119.1
Sales To Nwc (times)	6.2	4.8	4.4	7.9	5.4	4.6	8.2	6.5	4.1	12.5	7.0	3.5
Acct Pay To Sales (%)	5.0	6.7	8.5	7.4	8.1	9.4	3.3	7.7	9.3	4.0	6.2	8.7
PROFITABILITY												
Return On Sales (%)	7.2	2.9	0.1	10.0	7.2	5.9	7.4	2.7	1.9	10.3	6.4	2.3
Return On Assets (%)	14.5	7.2	0.4	11.6	9.2	4.8	14.5	8.5	3.4	13.8	9.1	2.8
Return On Nw (%)	21.3	13.2	1.4	21.0	18.6	15.9	48.6	26.1	12.7	30.2	18.0	10.0

	SIC 2869 IND ORG CHEM, NEC INDUSTRY ASSETS $1,000,000-$5,000,000 1997 (16 Establishments)			SIC 2869 IND ORG CHEM, NEC INDUSTRY ASSETS $5,000,000-$25,000,000 1997 (20 Establishments)			SIC 2873 NITROGENOUS FRTLZRS (NO BREAKDOWN) 1997 (42 Establishments)			SIC 2875 FRTLZRS, MIXING ONLY (NO BREAKDOWN) 1997 (49 Establishments)		
RATIOS	UQ	MED	LQ	UQ	MED	LQ	UQ	MED	LQ	UQ	MED	LQ
SOLVENCY												
Quick Ratio (times)	1.2	0.9	0.8	1.8	1.2	0.3	1.7	1.0	0.5	1.3	0.9	0.5
Current Ratio (times)	2.3	1.5	1.2	3.5	2.2	1.5	2.9	1.9	1.2	2.3	1.5	1.2
Curr Liab To Nw (%)	57.7	102.3	149.2	19.8	29.7	73.1	22.7	47.1	181.2	32.3	50.1	74.1
Curr Liab To Inv (%)	113.7	147.4	268.5	73.9	139.2	216.8	99.0	131.0	290.2	81.3	122.6	187.5
Total Liab To Nw (%)	66.6	146.0	290.1	20.6	49.7	100.4	25.3	85.8	193.1	43.6	82.4	194.8
Fixed Assets To Nw (%)	32.7	71.4	129.9	24.1	36.3	87.7	41.4	69.0	109.2	33.2	58.8	90.4
EFFICIENCY												
Coll Period (days)	36.4	46.2	64.4	33.3	42.0	55.7	14.2	31.4	55.9	21.9	28.1	44.2
Sales To Inv (times)	19.6	14.1	6.2	13.7	8.6	5.4	13.3	8.6	6.3	15.7	9.7	7.1
Assets To Sales (%)	46.7	49.5	76.8	46.3	60.7	88.2	42.8	76.1	88.1	29.8	43.0	51.8
Sales To Nwc (times)	24.0	8.5	5.0	8.7	4.6	1.6	8.2	4.8	3.0	14.3	7.9	4.8
Acct Pay To Sales (%)	2.6	4.8	8.6	3.4	6.3	7.9	2.6	6.2	9.1	3.4	5.2	6.9
PROFITABILITY												
Return On Sales (%)	7.7	4.6	1.4	10.8	7.3	1.5	9.1	3.9	2.3	3.1	1.6	0.4
Return On Assets (%)	11.2	7.5	2.0	16.2	12.0	0.4	14.8	8.8	1.2	7.7	2.7	0.5
Return On Nw (%)	28.3	18.4	9.9	25.2	18.9	0.9	65.4	17.0	3.6	18.2	8.5	2.0

This value is also good compared to the industry norm, 89.1 percent. For the debt-to-equity ratio, a slightly lower number is better.

Return-on-Equity Ratio. Profitability ratios tell the magnitude of profit a competitor is making versus others in its sector. Return on equity is the best known of all the profitability ratios. It is calculated as:

$$\frac{\text{Net income}}{\text{Total shareholder equity}}$$

Sample Inc.'s return-on-equity ratio is:

$$\text{NI/OE} = 300/6,900 = .043, \text{ or } 4.3\%$$

This value is low compared to the industry norm of 18 percent. (Dun & Bradstreet refers to this ratio as return on net worth.)

By calculating three common financial ratios you can quickly assess a competitor's financial strengths and weaknesses. If Sample Inc. were your competitor, it would be a financially sound and formidable foe.

Economic Value Added

Another indicator of a competitor's strength is its economic value added (EVA). A business must earn enough profit over time to compensate its stockholders for their willingness to provide money to the business. If the business exceeds stockholder expectation, value is added. The EVA metric is aligned with this basic premise. Investors' expected return is the minimum acceptable level of expected performance needed to get investors to provide capital, given the risks of actually realizing that performance. EVA is therefore an essential measure to calculate for your competitor. It will tell you if it is investing its stockholders' money wisely. This calculation basically asks: "You were supposed to earn so much money on your investment. Did you?" It is calculated as:

$$\text{EVA} = \text{Net income} - (\text{Cost of capital} \times \text{Net assets})$$

Net income is taken right from the income statement found in the annual report. Net investment is calculated from information found on the balance sheet of the annual report using the equations shown in Figure 7-8.

The cost of capital is the weighted average cost of financing from all sources (debt and equity). It is the percentage return that will allow the payment of debt and stockholder dividends. Your finance department should know this number. It has held pretty constant for most industries at around 12 percent for the last ten years. It's reasonable to assume that your competitor's cost of capital is the same as your own.

Suppose you want to size up one of your competitors, Magnum Industries. Extracting the necessary data from its income statement (Figure 7-9) and balance sheet (Figure 7-10), you obtain the EVA calculation shown in Figure 7-11.

Figure 7-11 shows that Magnum is not earning more than the cost of capital on all its assets. This competitor is not formidable. You can pursue aggressive strategies toward Magnum once you know your own product and process are both the best they can be and competitive.

Return on Net Assets

The last metric you should look at, not only for a competitor, but for your own company as well, is return on net

FIGURE 7-8.
Format for calculating net assets

FIGURE 7-9.

Income statement for Magnum Industries

Item	Transaction Amount (million $)	Balance (million $)
Revenue		20,000
– Cost of goods sold	15,000	
– General and administrative costs	2,500	
– Depreciation	500	
Subtotal of expenses	18,000	
Pretax income		2,000
Income taxes (40%)	800	
Net income		1,200

FIGURE 7-10.

Balance sheet for Magnum Industries

Assets (million $)		Liabilities (million $)	
Cash	1,000	Accounts payable	1,500
Accounts receivable	2,500	Short-term debt	1,000
Inventory	2,000		
Current assets	5,500	Current liabilities	2,500
Property, plant, and equipment	20,000		
– Accumulated depreciation	10,000		
	10,000		
		Stockholder's equity	13,000
	15,500		15,500

assets (RONA). To develop this metric you must understand fully all the operating and investment decisions your competitor makes on the whole as a company. This information, in addition to the EVA, will show the areas of financial strength and weakness due to your competitor's management philosophy. This information is invaluable when you set your company's business strategies.

FIGURE 7-11.

Calculation of economic value added (EVA) for Magnum Industries

Item (million $)		
Net income		1,200
+ Gross permanent investment	20,000	
– Accumulated depreciation	−10,000	
	10,000	
+ Net working capital	3,000	
Net investment	13,000	
× Cost of capital	× 12	
	1,560	
EVA		(360)
+ Current assets	5,500	
– Current liabilities	−2,500	
Net working capital		3,000

The calculation for RONA is:

RONA (%) = Net income margin × Investment turnover

In Figure 7-12, the far left-hand column shows operating decisions available to management that can ultimately affect RONA. The middle columns show performance elements controlled by the operating decisions. The far right-hand column shows the performance evaluation of net income margin and investment turnover that are used to calculate RONA. The RONA percentage may then be compared with the industry average to assess management's philosophy on running the company, which tells you how to set strategies against your competitor. If your competitor's RONA is higher than the industry norm, the company is well managed and positioned to take advantage of competitive weaknesses. If its RONA is lower than the industry norm, it might need to focus internally on its own business and therefore be unable to respond to a competitive threat.

FIGURE 7-12.
Return on net assets (RONA): underlying decisions

Decision Arena	Performance Elements	Performance Evaluation

OPERATING DECISIONS

INVESTMENT DECISIONS

The operating decisions available to management are:

- Pricing policy
- Product selection
- Geographic market selection
- Vendor selection
- Yield performance
- Operating budget
- Tax policy rates and tax benefits
- Accounts receivable policy and collection strategies
- Inventory policy and control
- Capital budgeting, expenditures, and commitments

Some of Magnum Industries' performance elements are available on its income statement and balance sheet. Total sales are $20,000 million.

Variable costs and controllable fixed costs cannot be ascertained from Magnum's income statement. However, we know that its total cash costs are a combination of:

- Cost of goods sold of $15,000 million
- General and administrative costs of $2,500 million
- Taxes of $800 million

These give total cash costs of $18,300 million. Gross operating investment is $24,500 million. This number comes from the balance sheet: $20,000 million gross permanent investment, $2,000 million inventory, and $2,500 million accounts receivable. There is $10,000 million of accumulated depreciation and $2,500 million of current liabilities.

To calculate the net income margin, divide the cash inflow (sales of $20,000 million minus total cash costs of $18,300 million) less depreciation ($500 million) by sales. This yields a net income margin of 6 percent.

To calculate investment turnover divide sales by total net assets (gross operating investment of $24,500 million minus $10,000 million of accumulated depreciation minus $2,500 million of current liabilities). This yields an investment turnover of 1.67.

Thus the RONA for Magnum Industries is:

$$\text{Net income margin} \times \text{Investment turnover}$$
$$= .06 \times 1.67 = .10 \ (10 \ \%)$$

A decent RONA for this industry is 13 percent. Magnum Industries, at 10 percent, is well below this figure and, therefore, is not a formidable competitor.

Magnum needs to increase its investment turnover or its net income margin. Some strategies to do that would be:

- Decreasing its total net assets by selling off some of its inventory, collecting receivables, and not investing in plants and equipment
- Increasing its cash inflow by reducing fixed and variable costs

Neither of these strategies is conducive to expanding product capacity or increasing market share. On the contrary, Magnum Industries must do some serious internal work before focusing externally. If Magnum Industries is your competitor, you can confidently take an aggressive strategy against them. (Granted this analysis is for the total company and is not product specific. However, it gives your company a general sense of the focus of Magnum Industries' management decisions.)

Resources Needed

Competitive assessments consume resources: people, dollars, and time spent gathering the data and preparing the analysis. Therefore, the extent of the assessment should be weighed against the impact the competitor or competitors have on the market. Spending $200,000 annually and forming a team of six people makes perfect sense if you are trying to assess and maintain a $40 million a year business. Your team could be made up of consultants, engineers, business strategies, economic evaluators, patents experts, your process technical person, R&D staff,

FIGURE 7-13.
Crossword puzzle

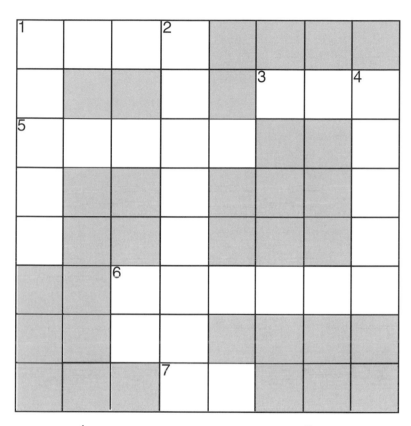

Across

1. Investment in $/lb. for new "Hytrend" product.

3. Big Mac Inc.'s solvent.

5. Big Mac Inc.'s filament surface finish.

6. Is Big Mac Inc.'s filament surface finish worse or better than yours?

7. Should your company be aggressive toward Big Mac Inc.'s planned expansion?

Down

1. Percent of the market share of "Hytrend" controlled by Big Mac Inc.?

2. Your estimate of Big Mac Inc.'s profit margin in percent.

4. Are Big Mac Inc.'s costs higher or lower than yours?

and product managers. Again, the amount of money spent and the proportion of people's time spent on the assessment will vary greatly depending on the importance management places on the final analysis.

Putting Together the Competitor's Picture

As I have already stated, having a good estimate of a competitor's products, processes, investment, cost structure, and cash flow is like filling in the words in a crossword puzzle. You take seemingly unrelated pieces of information and fit them together to form a complete picture. Fill out the crossword puzzle in Figure 7-13 using the data in the case study (the answers appear in Figure 7-14 at the end of the chapter).

Case Study: Competitive Assessment of Big Mac Inc.

You have read that your main competitor, Big Mac Inc., has announced that it is building a new plant in Lyman, South Carolina, to make Hytrend filament. The plant will have a capacity of 2 million pounds and will require an investment of $10 million.

Currently, the Hytrend market is shared by three competitors. Big Mac Inc. has 40 percent, your company has 35 percent, and XYZ has 25 percent of the market.

You feel this new capacity will allow Big Mac to lower its costs and raise its profit margin and market share. Hytrend sells for $9.44 per pound, and you think Big Mac's cost is $8 per pound, similar to yours.

To understand Big Mac's costs you hire a consultant to do a patent search and try to identify its process for making Hytrend. Your analysis shows that Big Mac's product and process differ from yours in two big areas, which you did not realize. Its patents say that it uses PDL solvent at $.50 per pound, which gives a rough surface to its filament. (You often

FIGURE 7-14.
Crossword puzzle with answers

¹F	I	V	²E				
O			I		³P	D	⁴L
⁵R	O	U	G	H			O
T			H				W
Y			T				E
		⁶B	E	T	T	E	R
			E				
			⁷N	O			

Across

1. Investment in $/lb. for new "Hytrend" product.

3. Big Mac Inc.'s solvent.

5. Big Mac Inc.'s filament surface finish.

6. Is Big Mac Inc.'s filament surface finish worse or better than yours?

7. Should your company be aggressive toward Big Mac Inc.'s planned expansion?

Down

1. Percent of the market share of "Hytrend" controlled by Big Mac Inc.?

2. Your estimate of Big Mac Inc.'s profit margin in percent.

4. Are Big Mac Inc.'s costs higher or lower than yours?

wondered how it obtained its excellent surface finish.) Your company puts the filament through an additional operation to mechanically scratch the surface, which costs an extra $.40 per pound, while you use HMEX solvent at $1.10 per pound.

Big Mac's process also apparently requires a heat-treating operation, needed because PDL solvent does not produce a strong filament. You estimate this adds $.75 per pound to its manufacturing costs.

After you have filled in all your answers, check the completed puzzle in Figure 7-14.

Appendix: Toyobo Patent

Translation
PATENT BUREAU OF JAPAN
Official Gazette for Unexamined Patents

Japanese Patent Application Publication Kokai: 2–80418

Publication Date: March 20, 1990

Number of Inventions: 1

Request of Examination: (Not yet requested). (Total of 6 pages)

International Class	Intrabureau
C 08 G18/10	7602–4J
18/65	7602–4J

A METHOD OF MANUFACTURING A
POLYURETHANE ELASTIC BODY

Application No.: 63–231244

Application Date: September 14, 1988

Inventors: K. Tani
                c/o General Research Laboratories
                Toyobo Company, Ltd.
                1-1 Katada 2-chome
                Otsu City, Shiga Prefecture

K. Katsuo
c/o Tsuruga Plant
Toyobo Company, Ltd.
10-24 Toyo-cho
Tsuruga City, Fukui Prefecture

H. Tagata
c/o Tsuruga Plant
Toyobo Company, Ltd.
10-24 Toyo-cho
Tsuruga City, Fukui Prefecture

Applicant: Toyobo Company, Ltd.
2-8 Dojimahama 2-chome
Kita-ku, Osaka City, Osaka Prefecture

Patent Attorney: H. Ueki

SPECIFICATION

1. **Title of the Invention**

A Method of Manufacturing a Polyurethane Elastic Body

2. **Claim**

A method of manufacturing a polyurethane elastic body which is a method of manufacturing a polyurethane elastic body by reacting a diol compound with a diisocyanate compound to obtain a prepolymer having isocyanate groups in its terminals and by reacting a diamine compound with the prepolymer to effect chain elongation characterized by the fact that the aforementioned prepolymer is separated into at least two groups and that chain elongation is initiated by reacting the aforementioned diamine compound with one of these groups, after which the prepolymer of the remaining group is mixed at any desired time and a further chain elongation reaction is performed.

3. **Detailed Description of the Invention**

(Sphere of industrial use)

This invention relates to an improved method of manufacturing a polyurethane elastic body in which a diol compound is reacted with an excess number of moles of a diisocyanate compound to obtain a prepolymer and in which the prepolymer is subjected to chain elongation with a diamine compound, and, in particular, to a method for effecting a chain elongation of the aforementioned prepolymer in an optimum state.

(Conventional technology)

Polyuretane elastic bodies are obtained by additional polymerization of diol compounds and diisocyanate compounds. As a continuous manufacture procedure, the diol compound and the diisocyanate compound are reacted in a first reaction apparatus to obtain a prepolymer having isocyanate groups in its terminals, the prepolymer then being dissolved in an inactive polar organic solvent, afer which said prepolymer solution is introduced into a second reaction apparatus, with polymer chain extension being performed in the second reaction apparatus by supplying a diamine compound (chain elongation agent and with a polyurethane elastic body being obtained. This type of manufacturing method can be seen, for example, in the examples of U.S. Patent No. 3,557,044. As required, a monoamine compound can be supplied as a terminal termination agent together with the chain elongation agent. Polytetramethylene glycol, for example, is used as the aforementioned diol compound and p,p-diphenyl-methanediisocyanate, for example, is used as the diisocyanate compound.

STEP 3:

SET TARGET COST AND IDENTIFY AREAS TO IMPROVE

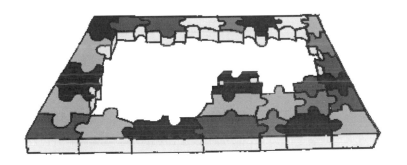

8

COST TARGETING AND
PROCESS IMPROVEMENT

Before you begin to identify areas that need attention and implement programs that will improve your company's cost picture, you first need to estimate competitor costs and compare them with your company's actual costs.

Figure 8-1 gives fictitious costs for your competitor and your company. Look at the seven major areas of cost. Determine where your competitor's strengths are. If you picked materials, labor, and overheads, you are correct! Your competitor has a $.70 per pound advantage in materials, a $.40 per pound advantage in labor, and a $.30 per pound advantage in overhead costs.

Your company's best strategy is to make plans to improve these areas. If your plans come up short, or you don't believe your company can drastically reduce these costs, then the best strategy might be to not spend any R&D money on this project, or maybe to use this product as a cash cow and not plan to reinvest. If, on the other hand, your R&D team can identify ways to reduce these costs below your competitor's, then the expenditure to protect this market will be worthwhile. However, I do recommend that a full cash flow analysis be done before proceeding. This analysis will ensure that the investment yields an appropriate return.

If your competitor's weak areas are utilities, maintenance, and depreciation, property taxes, and insurance, what does this

FIGURE 8-1.
Fictitious costs

Item	Competitive Costs ($/lb)	Your Costs ($/lb)
Materials used	0.80	1.50
Utilities	0.06	0.02
Labor	1.60	2.00
Maintenance	0.25	0.10
Depreciation, property taxes, and insurance	0.80	0.50
Plant overheads	1.20	1.50
	4.71	5.62
General and administrative costs	0.70	0.75
	5.41	6.37

tell you? These are the three areas directly related to total investment. Your competitor must have more automation or a new or more streamlined process than yours. You can determine how much larger your competitor's total investment is than your company's by using the equation for depreciation, property taxes, and insurance. Knowing your competitor's volume and yours, and knowing your investment, you can calculate your competitor's total investment. The formula to estimate depreciation, property taxes, and insurance is:

(DTI) Depreciation, property taxes, and insurance
= .11 × Total investment (TI)

If your competitor makes a million pounds of this product, its depreciation, property taxes, and insurance costs are:[1]

DTI = $.80/lb × 1 million lb = $800,000

Total investment can then be calculated as:

---

1. $.80 per pound is the competition's DTI cost.

$$DTI = .11 \times TI$$
$$TI \ \ = DTI/.11$$
$$TI \ \ = \$800,000/.11 = \$8.8 \text{ million}$$

If your company is also producing a million pounds of product, your investment is:

$$DTI = \$.50/lb \times 1 \text{ million lb} = \$500,000$$
$$TI \ \ = \$500,000/.11 = \$5.5 \text{ million}$$

You can see that your competitor's process requires $3.3 million more to make the product than your company's, or 66 percent more investment. But look at the ramifications if it spends that amount. Its material costs are 50 percent of yours, and its labor is 20 percent less.

This calculation is very informative because you now have some standard by which to judge spending necessitated by identified plans to reduce materials and labor costs. It basically shows you what you can afford to spend to be in line with your competition.

The Strategic Costing Process, however, is not just about being as good as your competition; rather it's about being the "best of the best." That means your challenge to your R&D personnel is to identify programs or process changes that produce a cost sheet *lower* than your competitors!

In our example, management and R&D personnel prepare the target cost sheet shown in Figure 8-2. Target costs are lower than the competitor's in the area of labor but slightly higher for materials. By comparing the target cost sheet with your company's actual cost sheet, we calculate the "change" column (subtracting your company's actual costs from the target costs).

The major areas targeted for improvement are materials, total investment, and labor. In our example, the area most in need of improvement is labor. The differences between target cost and actual cost are $.50 per pound for direct labor and $.37 per pound for overheads, which we have related to labor. Therefore, by meeting your target costs, you reduce labor and overheads by

FIGURE 8-2.
Target cost sheet

Item	Target Costs ($/lb)	Change ($/lb)
Materials used	0.90	–0.60
Utilities	0.05	+0.03
Labor	1.50	–0.50
Maintenance	0.20	+0.10
Depreciation, property taxes, and insurance	0.75	+0.25
Plant overheads	1.13	–0.37
General and administrative costs	0.68	–0.07
	5.21	–1.16

$.87 per pound. This is better than your competitor's estimated cost sheet.

Likewise, $.60 per pound is projected to be saved on materials, and $.38 per pound can be spent on new investment to accomplish these goals.

As we move into the next phase of analysis, we actually begin the second part of step 3. Part one, setting target costs, doesn't accomplish much unless you go on to identify areas that need improvement. Figure 8-3 lists differences between your business and your competitor's. It identifies three areas where differences have been noted then gives several plans for improving these areas where you are lacking. This is how you actually begin making plans to improve your processes.

R&D should then identify even more specific areas to improve in order to accomplish your goals as stated in Figure 8-3. This completes the cycle and, if successful, elevates your company to a more competitive level against your competition. This position allows your company to implement proactive and aggressive strategies.

Strategic costing requires you to identify areas to improve, to analyze the effort needed to accomplish those goals (investment and time), and calculate the value to the firm of achieving the

FIGURE 8-3.
Areas to improve

Area 1: Labor (–0.87)
- Look into process improvement
- Look into streamlined and efficient operation
- Look into training for higher productivity

Area 2: Materials (–0.60)
- Look into process yields and waste
- Look into material prices (negotiate with suppliers)

Area 3: Investment (+0.38)
- Invest more in process to gain improvements in other areas

---

improvements. Calculating the value to the firm, using cash flow analysis, is the subject of Chapter 9.

The Strategic Costing Process can be used, not only to plan your strategies for achieving lower costs than your competitors, but also to revisit your cost position frequently to make sure that once your company is on top, it stays on top by continuously improving. Today the marketplace is changing rapidly, sometimes daily. Strategic costing allows you to keep up with the changes, not only locally, but globally.

STEP 4:

CALCULATE THE VALUE TO YOUR COMPANY OF THE STRATEGIC COSTING PROCESS

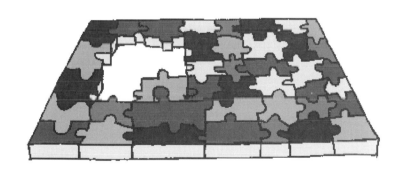

9

ADDING VALUE TO
YOUR COMPANY

Any changes your company considers making must be viewed in terms of not only short-term rewards but also long-term effects. To see the effect of your suggested changes on your company's financial status over time, we will look at ten years of discounted cash flow. Cumulative discounted cash flow yields a more complete picture than just net profit.

Cash flow also includes depreciation and any investments made to increase your company's competitiveness. Looking at cash flow over time and discounting later-year cash streams to the present will put all cash streams in terms of today's dollars. Cumulating these discounted cash flow streams gives the net present value (NPV). NPV is an economic measure of merit. If the NPV is positive, your investment has earned a certain percentage (that at which the stream was discounted, or the cost of capital) per year plus an additional amount.

Cash Flow

The flow of cash through a business is like the flow of blood through the human body. If a person severs an artery, the bleeding must be stopped—the quicker, the better. If the bleeding is allowed to continue unheeded, debilitation comes first, then death. If the bleeding is stopped before death occurs, a blood transfusion must be given in order to restore the person's stamina. Cash is just as vital to a business as blood to the body. If more cash flows out of the business than flows in, the business will be unhealthy, and may even die. This cash "anemia" is especially common among smaller businesses, which typically do not have large reserves of cash. Cash flow analysis may be used to determine a business's health and to develop financial plans. Also, knowing your competitor's projected cash flow allows your company's long-range strategies to be proactive. Knowing levels of cash flow is critical during expansion phases.

Cash flow is the sum of money coming into the business minus outflow. The main source of cash inflow is sales revenue. To a lesser extent cash could also come from the sale of equipment or technology. Figure 9-1 is a graphical representation of the flow of cash through the business. The cash inflow from sales revenues is depicted as a large artery.

Outflows are all cash expenses necessary to operate the business, costs for new permanent facilities or equipment, and taxes. Cash expenses include the seven main costs described in Chapter 3: materials used, labor, utilities, maintenance, overheads, depreciation, taxes, and insurance, and general and administrative costs. After cash expenses are deducted, the resultant flow of money is considered income after expenses.

Let's examine a hypothetical business, Quality Build Construction. Quality Build completed seven jobs during the year for a total cash inflow of $75,000. Cash expenses were as follows:

Labor (salary, wages, taxes, and benefits)	$17,500
Material purchases	12,500
Supplies	3,000
Utilities	0
Rent	0
Interest paid on loans	4,000
Property taxes	3,000
Advertising	1,000
	$41,000

FIGURE 9-1.
Cash flow through a company

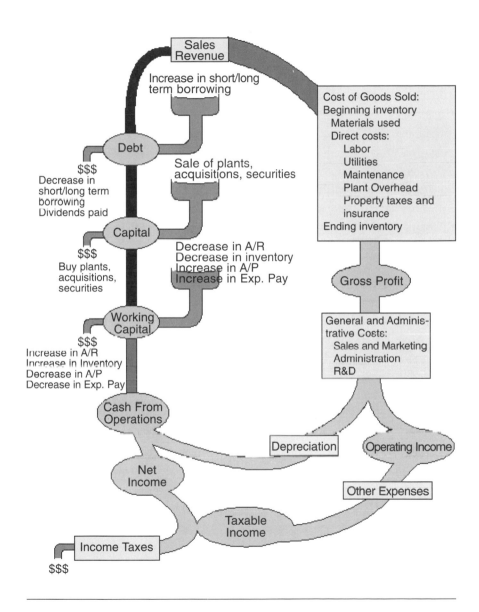

Thus Quality Build had cash inflows of $75,000 minus $41,000 in cash expenses, or income after expenses of $34,000.

The next drain on cash is taxes, which usually total around 40 percent for both federal and state taxes. However, taxes are not paid on income until allowances are deduced, since the government assists businesses by giving an allowance on purchase of new facilities and equipment. This allowance is called depreciation. Depreciation is a certain percentage of the cost of equipment or facilities that can be deducted from income after expenses. This percentage is usually based on the life of the equipment. Typically, the useful life of equipment is ten years, so 10 percent of the equipment's value can, therefore, be deducted as depreciation each year for ten years. Taxable income is calculated by deducting depreciation from income after expenses. If Quality Build has just purchased new equipment for $50,000, it can be depreciated at $5,000 per year for ten years. Quality Build's taxable income is income after expenses of $34,000 minus depreciation of $5,000, or $29,000. In our example, Quality Build then pays taxes (assumed to be 40 percent) on $29,000, or $11,600. This would give the company after-tax income of $29,000 minus $11,600, or $17,400.

At this point, depreciation must be added back to the cash flow. The new sum is $22,400 ($17,400 + $5,000) and is called cash from operations. With cash from operations the owners can change working capital, pay off debts, or reinvest in the business by buying equipment or facilities. If assets are bought, these must be subtracted from cash from operations to yield the year's cash flow. The cash flow through Quality Build is summarized in Figure 9-2.

By plotting either actual or projected cash inflows minus outflows on a yearly basis, you can develop a plan to keep your business's finances running smoothly. "Cash flow is a yardstick used in recent years because it offers a better indication of the ability of a company to pay off debt or finance expansions from self-generated cash," says Frank Stermole in his book *Economic Evaluation and Investment Decisions Methods*.

FIGURE 9-2.
Calculation of cash flow

Revenue	$75,000
– Cash expenses	–41,000
Income after expenses	$34,000
– Depreciation	–5,000
Taxable income	$29,000
– Taxes	–11,600
After-tax income	$17,400
+ Depreciation	+5,000
Cash from operations	$22,400
– Capital investment	–50,000
Cash flow	(27,600)

By projecting cash flow for both your company and your competitor, you can get a financial picture of the effect of your strategic plan.

Net Present Value

To make sure you are comparing apples to apples, you must discount later-year cash flow streams to the present. Money can be invested to yield a profit, so a dollar in hand today is worth more than a dollar received in the future. By discounting future sums of money, today's value can be computed.

Take the following year-end cash flow:

End of year 1:	–1,000,000
	2:	–500,000
	3:	500,000
	4:	1,000,000
	5:	2,000,000

FIGURE 9-3.
Calculation of cumulative discounted cash flow

Cash Flow (thousand $)		Present Value Factor		Discounted Cash Flow	Cumulative Discounted Cash Flow
−1,000	×	0.870	=	−870	−870
−500	×	0.756	=	−378	−1,248
500	×	0.658	=	329	−919
1,000	×	0.572	=	572	−347
2,000	×	0.497	=	994	+647

Today's value of this cash stream can be calculated using discount factors, based on a certain discount percentage found in any accounting book's present value tables. (See the appendix for an example. Note that one dollar today is only worth about 30 cents ten years from now when using a 12 percent discount rate.)

Assuming a 15 percent discount rate, the present value for these five years of cash flow for the company is $647,000. The calculation is shown in Figure 9-3.

Case Study: IBC Company's Use of Ten-Year Cash Flow to Set Strategic Plans

IBC Company controls 65 percent of the lawn tractor market. Costs for an average fifteen-horsepower tractor are shown in Figure 9-4.

Last year, IBC Company sold one million tractors at $2,000 each and had a cash flow of $850 million (Figure 9-5). IBC made no new investments last year, but it still had $250 million worth of depreciation.

Larry W., IBC's controller, is asked to show the effect of IBC's long-range business strategy for the next ten years using inputs from finance, sales, engineering, and purchasing.

IBC Company's strategy is:

FIGURE 9-4.
Cost estimate for IBC Company

PROJECTED TOTAL COSTS, of

15 HP Tractors

COS, © 1989, Dale Brethauer

BASIC PREMISES:

Number of Operators:	1350
Hourly Wage Rate:	$19.5
Material Price:	$375.00
Process Yield:	95%
Sales Volume:	1,000,000
Total Investment:	$205,000,000

	$/YEAR	$/PIECE
VARIABLE COST		
Materials	$394,736,842	$394.74
Utilities	$4,100,000	$4.10
Subtotal Variable Costs	$398,836,842	$398.84
FIXED COSTS		
Labor	$126,341,640	$126.34
Equipment Maintenance	$12,300,000	$12.30
Overhead	$94,756,230	$94.76
Property Taxes and Insurance	$2,050,000	$2.05
Equipment Allocations	$20,500,000	$20.50
Subtotal Fixed Costs	$255,947,870	$255.95
SUBTOTAL VARIABLE AND FIXED COSTS	$654,784,712	$654.78
GENERAL AND ADMINISTRATIVE COSTS		
Selling Expense	$32,739,236	$32.74
Administration	$32,739,236	$32.74
Distribution	$32,739,236	$32.74
TOTAL COSTS	$753,002,419	$753.00

FIGURE 9-5.
Calculation of cash for IBC Company

Revenue (million $)	$2,000
– Cash expenses	750
– Depreciation	250
Taxable income	$1,000
– Taxes (40%)	400
After-tax income	$ 600
+ Depreciation	250
– Capital investment	0
Cash flow	$ 850

- After two years, when depreciation will be at zero, begin an automation project aimed at reducing cash expenses by 33 percent. This project will cost $2.5 billion.
- Sales will be steady, but increase 15 percent per year in two years due to a 10 percent reduction in selling price (25 percent below the competition).

The sales department, therefore, projects the sales outlined in Figure 9-6. The engineering department confirms that cash expenses can be reduced to $500 per unit; therefore, projected cash expenses are as shown in Figure 9-7.

Using this information, Larry's ten-year cash flow projection and discounted stream for the IBC Company shows a value to the company of $5,665 million in today's dollars. The details are outlined in Figure 9-8.

Larry has previously done a ten-year cash flow projection for IBC's major competitor, which had a value of $4,400 million in today's dollars. If IBC Company does not undertake the automation project to become more competitive, its sales will probably increase 3 percent per year. This growth results in a value of $4,778 million as seen in Figure 9-9.

By automating its process, IBC—rather than merely keeping even—gains compared to its main competitor. Larry's analysis confirms management's decision to proceed with this project.

Do you see how important these calculations are to the life of your company? They can make all the difference in business

FIGURE 9-6.
Sales forecast for IBC Company

Year	Volume (thousand)	Price per Unit ($)	Revenue (million $)
1	1,000	2,000	2,000
2	1,000	2,000	2,000
3	1,150	1,800	2,070
4	1,323	1,800	2,381
5	1,521	1,800	2,738
6	1,749	1,800	3,148
7	2,011	1,800	3,620
8	2,313	1,800	4,164
9	2,660	1,800	4,788
10	3,059	1,800	5,506

FIGURE 9-7.
Cash expense forecast for IBC Company

Year	Volume (thousand)	Cash Expenses per Unit ($)	Cash Expenses (million $)
1	1,000	750	750
2	1,000	750	750
3	1,150	500	575
4	1,323	500	661
5	1,521	500	760
6	1,749	500	875
7	2,011	500	1,006
8	2,313	500	1,157
9	2,660	500	1,330
10	3,059	500	1,530

decisions that determine how strong a competitor you can be, and many times, they have kept companies from having to go out of business![1]

---

1. Ten-year cash flow and NPV may be automatically calculated by using the Cash Flow Analysis spreadsheet found on the disk.

FIGURE 9-8.
Ten-year cash flow for IBC Company

Item	Year									
	1	2	3	4	5	6	7	8	9	10
Revenue	2,000	2,000	2,070	2,381	2,738	3,148	3,620	4,164	4,788	5,506
Other income										
Total revenue	2,000	2,000	2,070	2,381	2,738	3,148	3,620	4,164	4,788	5,506
– Cash expenses	750	750	575	661	760	875	1,006	1,157	1,330	1,530
– Depreciation	250	250	250	250	250	250	250	250	250	250
Taxable income	1,000	1,000	1,245	1,470	1,728	2,023	2,364	2,757	3,208	3,726
– Income taxes (40%)	400	400	498	588	691	809	946	1,103	1,283	1,490
Net income	600	600	747	882	1,037	1,214	1,418	1,654	1,925	2,236
+ Depreciation	250	250	250	250	250	250	250	250	250	250
– Investments			2,500							
Cash flow	850	850	(1,503)	1,132	1,287	1,464	1,668	1,904	2,175	2,486
Discount factor (12%)	0.893	0.797	0.712	0.636	0.567	0.507	0.452	0.404	0.36	0.322
Discounted cash flow	759	677	(1,070)	720	730	742	754	769	783	800
Cumulative discounted cash flow	759	1,437	366	1,086	1,816	2,558	3,312	4,081	4,864	5,665

FIGURE 9-9.

Ten-year cash flow without automation for IBC Company

Item	Year									
	1	2	3	4	5	6	7	8	9	10
Revenue	2,000	2,000	2,060	2,122	2,185	2,251	2,319	2,388	2,460	2,534
Other income										
Total revenue	2,000	2,000	2,060	2,122	2,185	2,251	2,319	2,388	2,388	2,534
– Cash expenses	750	750	773	796	820	844	869	896	922	950
– Depreciation	250	250	0	0	0	0	0	0	0	0
Taxable income	1,000	1,000	1,288	1,366	1,366	1,407	1,449	1,493	1,537	1,583
– Income taxes (40%)	400	400	515	530	546	563	580	597	615	633
Net income	600	600	773	796	820	844	869	896	922	950
+ Depreciation	250	250	0	0	0	0	0	0	0	0
– Investments										
Cash flow	850	850	773	796	820	844	869	896	922	950
Discount factor (12%)	0.893	0.797	0.712	0.636	0.567	0.507	0.452	0.404	0.36	0.322
Discounted cash flow	759	677	550	506	465	428	393	362	332	306
Cumulative discounted cash flow	759	1,437	1,987	2,493	2,957	3,385	3,778	4,140	4,472	4,778

Appendix: Present Value Table

Periods

(N)	4%	6%	8%	10%	12%	15%	20%	30%	50%
1	0.9615	0.9434	0.9259	0.9091	0.8929	0.8696	0.8333	0.7692	0.6667
2	0.9246	0.8900	0.8573	0.8264	0.7972	0.7561	0.6944	0.5917	0.4444
3	0.8890	0.8396	0.738	0.7513	0.7118	0.6575	0.5787	0.4552	0.2963
4	0.8548	0.7921	0.7350	0.6830	0.6355	0.5718	0.4823	0.3501	0.1975
5	0.8218	0.7473	0.6806	0.6209	0.5674	0.4972	0.4019	0.2693	0.1317
6	0.7903	0.7050	0.6302	0.5645	0.5066	0.4323	0.3349	0.2072	0.0878
7	0.7599	0.6651	0.5835	0.5132	0.4523	0.3759	0.2791	0.1594	0.0585
8	0.7307	0.6274	0.5403	0.4665	0.4039	0.3269	0.2326	0.1226	0.0390
9	0.7026	0.5919	0.5002	0.4241	0.3606	0.2843	0.1938	0.0943	0.0260
10	0.6756	0.5584	0.4632	0.3855	0.3220	0.2472	0.1615	0.0725	0.0173
11	0.6496	0.5268	0.4289	0.3505	0.2875	0.2149	0.1346	0.0558	0.0116
12	0.6246	0.4970	0.3971	0.3186	0.2567	0.1869	0.1122	0.0429	0.0077
13	0.6006	0.4688	0.3677	0.2897	0.2292	0.1625	0.0935	0.0330	0.0051
14	0.5775	0.4423	0.3405	0.2633	0.2046	0.1413	0.0779	0.0254	0.0034
15	0.5553	0.4173	0.3152	0.2394	0.1827	0.1229	0.0649	0.0195	0.0023
16	0.5339	0.3936	0.2919	0.2176	0.1631	0.1069	0.0541	0.0150	0.0015
17	0.5134	0.3714	0.2703	0.1978	0.1456	0.0929	0.0451	0.0116	0.0010
18	0.4936	0.3503	0.2502	0.1799	0.1300	0.0808	0.0376	0.0089	0.0007
19	0.4746	0.3305	0.2327	0.1635	0.1161	0.0703	0.0313	0.0068	0.0005
20	0.4564	0.3118	0.2145	0.1486	0.1037	0.0612	0.0261	0.0053	0.0003
25	0.3751	0.2330	0.1460	0.0923	0.0588	0.0304	0.0105	0.0014	
30	0.3083	0.1741	0.0994	0.0573	0.0334	0.0151	0.0042	0.0004	
40	0.2083	0.0972	0.0460	0.0221	0.0107	0.0037	0.0007		
50	0.1407	0.0543	0.0213	0.0085	0.0035	0.009	0.0001		

THE STRATEGIC COSTING PROCESS IN ACTION

10

PUTTING IT
ALL TOGETHER

In Chapters 2 through 9, we went through the strategic costing system step by step, putting all the pieces of the cost picture together. Let's reiterate the steps:

1. Estimate your suppliers' costs.
2. Estimate your competitors' costs.
3. Set your company's target cost sheet and identify areas for process and product improvement.
4. Determine the value to your company of making process and product changes and continuously improving.

In this chapter, we work through a real-life case study, with your role being a member of a team that will use the strategic costing system to set strategic goals for AMEX Company.

Case Study: AMEX Company

You work for AMEX Company, a very profitable medium-size high-technology manufacturing company. AMEX Company produces eleven different medical products and last year had annual sales of $100 million. One of its most profitable products has been a blood diagnostic instrument called DiaOs. AMEX was the first

company to bring this product to market, and while DiaOs sales
have increased steadily since its introduction in 1979, the price
has been dropping. All DiaOs patents have expired, and competition market share has been increasing steadily.

You are assigned by Bill Harns, production vice-president, to
be part of a team working to ensure that the DiaOs instrument
maintains optimal financial performance for the next ten years.
Bill recently attended an AMA seminar on strategic costing and
has hired a consultant to teach your team the methodology of
strategic costing and to facilitate your team's effort. He requests
that your team develop a target cost sheet for DiaOs, outline
R&D programs to reach your goals of optimal financial performance, list necessary capital investments, and calculate the NPV
of your team's strategic plan. Bill wants this analysis so he can
review it with Mike Smith, AMEX Company's CEO, during their
quarterly planning meeting.

AMEX Product and Financial Information for DiaOs Instrument

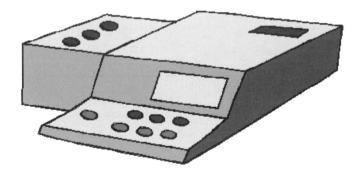

DiaOs Instrument Product Offering. DiaOs is a tabletop blood
diagnostic instrument. Blood is loaded by injection into the
instrument, which is then capable of running up to 27 diagnostic readings. The total length of test run time varies according to the number of tests conducted but averages 30 seconds
per test.

DiaOs replaces manual testing, which takes up to 5 minutes per test and sometimes results in inaccurate readings. DiaOs usually lasts five years and carries a two-year warranty. Reagents used to test the blood are contained within the instrument. They will last for well over 50 million tests and usually do not need to be replaced. There is one pound of reagent per instrument.

DiaOs Annual Sales. Figure 10-1 shows DiaOs sales since introduction, instruments sold each year, and annual revenues for each year.

Competition and Market Share. One instrument can usually satisfy the testing requirements of a large hospital. The total market for blood diagnostic instruments can be seen in Figure 10-2, along with the major competitors and their market shares, shown in units sold.

Process Flow Sheet. Figure 10-3 is a process flow sheet showing the steps in the manufacture of the instrument. Note that next to the boxes are three numbers; these numbers represent the number of operators per year, total capital investment, and the materials used for each process step.

Now let's look at the DiaOs cost sheet in Figure 10-4. Projected total costs are $180.78, with a selling price of $200. Materials are $68.42, which represents 33 percent of total costs. Knowing your supplier costs and working to reduce this area will ultimately have a huge impact on AMEX Company's competitiveness.

With all this product and financial information on the DiaOs instrument, your team is ready to proceed with the Strategic Costing Process to set strategic plans for the AMEX Company.

Step 1 is to estimate AMEX supplier costs.

Referring to the process flow diagram (Figure 10-3), you see four major necessary materials:

FIGURE 10-1.
Annual sales for AMEX DiaOs instrument

Years Since Introduction	Units Sold (thousand)	Price	Annual Revenue
1	10	$500	$5,000,000
2	12	$500	$6,000,000
3	14	$450	$6,300,000
4	16	$450	$7,200,000
5	18	$425	$7,650,000
6	20	$400	$8,000,000
7	23	$375	$8,625,000
8	26	$325	$8,450,000
9	29	$300	$8,700,000
10	32	$275	$8,800,000
11	35	$250	$8,750,000
12	38	$225	$8,550,000
13	41	$225	$9,225,000
14	44	$200	$8,800,000
15	47	$200	$9,400,000
16	50	$200	$10,000,000
17	50	$200	$10,000,000

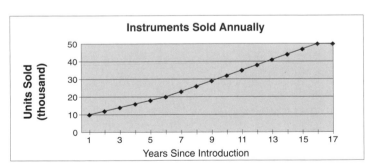

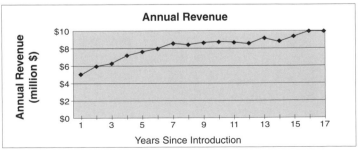

FIGURE 10-2.
Total market information

Years Since	Units Sold (thousand)		
Introduction	AMEX	Chockton	Meds
1	10		
2	12		
3	14		
4	16		
5	18		
6	20		
7	23	5	
8	26	8	
9	29	11	
10	32	14	
11	35	17	
12	38	20	
13	41	17	10
14	44	18	20
15	47	23	30
16	50	25	40
17	50	25	50

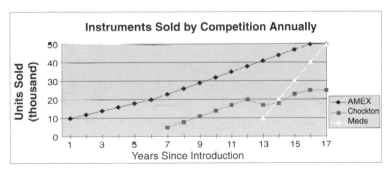

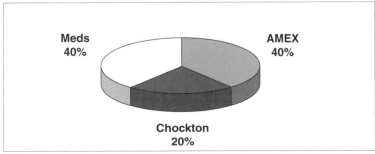

FIGURE 10-3.

Process flow diagram for AMEX DiaOs instrument

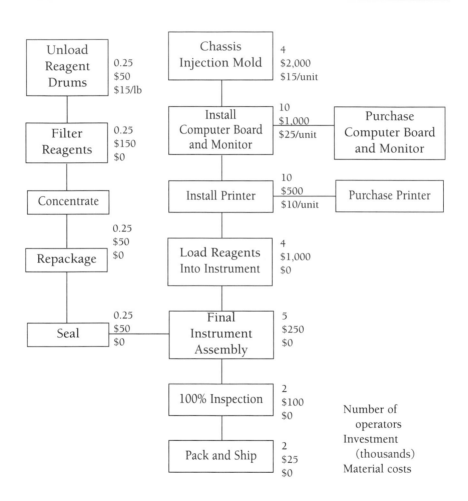

Number of
  operators
Investment
  (thousands)
Material costs

FIGURE 10-4.
Cost estimate for AMEX

PROJECTED TOTAL COSTS, of

AMEX Instrument Costs

COS, © 1989, Dale Brethauer

BASIC PREMISES:

Number of Operators:	38
Hourly Wage Rate:	$15.00
Material Price:	$65.00
Process Yield:	95%
Sales Volume:	65,000
Total Investment:	$5,175,000

	$/YEAR	$/PIECE
VARIABLE COST		
Materials	$4,447,368	$68.42
Utilities	$103,500	$1.59
Subtotal Variable Costs	$4,550,868	$70.01
FIXED COSTS		
Labor	$2,735,602	$42.09
Equipment Maintenance	$310,500	$4.78
Overhead	$2,051,702	$31.56
Property Taxes and Insurance	$51,750	$0.80
Equipment Allocations	$517,500	$7.96
Subtotal Fixed Costs	$5,667,054	$87.19
SUBTOTAL VARIABLE AND FIXED COSTS	$10,217,923	$157.20
GENERAL AND ADMINISTRATIVE COSTS		
Selling Expense	$510,896	$7.86
Administration	$510,896	$7.86
Distribution	$510,896	$7.86
TOTAL COSTS	$11,750,611	$180.78

FIGURE 10-5.
Reduction in material costs for AMEX

Component	Supplier	Component Cost	Estimated Cost	Potential Reduction	Comment
Chassis	Ny-Ex	$15/unit	$15.00	$7.50	Use second quality plastic at $.50/lb
Reagent	Gupe Company	$15/lb	$10.75	$4.25	Negotiate to at least $12.50/lb
Computer board, monitor, and printer	Master Associates	$35/unit	$32	$25	In-house production

1. Injection-molded chassis at $15/unit
2. Reagent at $15/lb
3. Computer boards and monitor at $25/unit
4. Printer at $10/unit

After visiting three suppliers' facilities, your team estimates the costs and negotiable reductions shown in Figure 10-5. (All cost estimates can be found in the appendix: Figures 10A-1, 10A-2, and 10A-3.) Would you have identified the same areas of cost reductions in preparation for negotiations?

Step 2 is to estimate your competitors' cost sheets. AMEX Company's main competitors are Meds Company and Chockton Inc. Even though Meds Company is the most recent entrant, it has captured 40 percent of the market. Your competitive studies show Meds to be very modern with a highly automated process. Its total investment is estimated at about $1.5 million more than AMEX, with an estimated twelve fewer operators. Its estimated cost sheet (Figure 10A-4 in the appendix) shows a cost of $153.12 per unit, versus AMEX's cost of $180.78 per unit. Chockton has never been perceived as a formidable competitor, and a study of that company bears this assessment out. It has a low-technology operation that is labor intensive. Its estimated cost sheet (Figure 10A-5 in the appendix) shows a cost of $408.10 per unit.

Step 3 begins with a comparison of the AMEX cost sheet

FIGURE 10-6.
Target costs for AMEX

Item	AMEX ($/instrument)	Meds ($/instrument)	Variance	Chockton ($/instrument)	Variance	Target Cost
Variable costs						
Materials used	68.42	57.89	(10.53)	68.42	0.00	55.00
Utilities	1.59	2.18	0.59	3.10	1.51	2.00
Fixed costs						
Labor	42.09	31.20	(10.89)	146.88	104.79	30.00
Maintenance	4.78	6.53	1.75	9.30	4.52	5.50
Plant overheads	31.57	23.40	(8.17)	110.16	78.59	22.50
Depreciation, property taxes, and insurance	8.76	11.96	3.29	17.05	8.29	10.00
Cost of manufacture	157.21	133.16	(24.05)	354.91	197.70	125.00
General and administrative costs						
Selling expenses	7.86	5.66	(1.20)	17.75	9.89	6.25
Administration	7.86	5.66	(1.20)	17.75	9.89	6.25
Distribution	7.86	5.66	(1.20)	17.75	9.89	6.25
Total costs	180.79	153.14	(27.65)	408.16	227.37	143.75
Selling price	200.00	17.500	(25.00)	435.00	235.00	175.00
Profit	19.21	21.86		26.84		31.25
Profit margin (%)	11	14		7		22

with the estimated cost sheets of Meds and Chockton. If we lay the AMEX cost sheet next to those for the two major competitors, we can review the variances, as illustrated in Figure 10-6.

Step 3 continues with the identification of major areas for process and product improvement that will accomplish the target cost goal of $143.75 per unit. The two major areas are materials and labor, with projected reductions in cost of $13.42 per unit for materials and $12.09 per unit for labor. To achieve these goals, the following programs are identified:

- Use second-quality plastic for the chassis.
- Negotiate a $2.50 per pound reduction in reagent costs.
- Investigate in-house production of the computer board, monitor, and printer.
- Further automate the instrument assembly procedure.

If these programs are successful the DiaOs instrument could have costs below $145. This reduction would enable AMEX to again be the market leader in blood diagnostic instruments.

Step 4 is to determine the value to the company of implementing these process and product improvements. Assuming success in all four programs, a ten-year cash flow analysis shows a cost reduction of $35 per unit, a regain of market share at 5 percent per year growth, and a competitive price of $175 per unit. These changes yield a very attractive NPV of $12 million (see Figures 10A-6 and 10A-7 in the appendix). For this analysis it was estimated that a capital investment in automation of $2 million would be required.

This concludes a very successful application of the strategic costing system.

Appendix: Calculations

Supplier Cost Sheets

FIGURE 10A-1.
Cost estimate for Ny-Ex chassis

PROJECTED TOTAL COSTS, of

Ny-Ex Chassis

COS, © 1989, Dale Brethauer

BASIC PREMISES:

Number of Operators:	1
Hourly Wage Rate:	$12.50
Material Price:	$9.00
Process Yield:	90%
Sales Volume:	60,000
Total Investment:	$400,000

	$/YEAR	$/PIECE
VARIABLE COST		
Materials	$600,000	$10.00
Utilities	$8,000	$0.13
Subtotal Variable Costs	$608,000	$10.13
FIXED COSTS		
Labor	$59,991	$1.00
Equipment Maintenance	$24,000	$0.40
Overhead	$44,993	$0.75
Property Taxes and Insurance	$4,000	$0.07
Equipment Allocations	$40,000	$0.67
Subtotal Fixed Costs	$172,985	$2.88
SUBTOTAL VARIABLE AND FIXED COSTS	$780,985	$13.02
GENERAL AND ADMINISTRATIVE COSTS		
Selling Expense	$39,049	$0.65
Administration	$39,049	$0.65
Distribution	$39,049	$0.65
TOTAL COSTS	$898,132	$14.97

FIGURE 10A-2.

Cost estimate for Gupe Company reagent

PROJECTED TOTAL COSTS, of

Gupe Co. Reagents

COS, © 1989, Dale Brethauer

BASIC PREMISES:

Number of Operators:	2
Hourly Wage Rate:	$11.67
Material Price:	$9.00
Process Yield:	95%
Sales Volume:	60,000
Total Investment:	$100,000

	$/YEAR	$/PIECE
VARIABLE COST		
Materials	$568,421	$9.47
Utilities	$2,000	$0.03
Subtotal Variable Costs	$570,421	$9.51
FIXED COSTS		
Labor	$112,016	$1.87
Equipment Maintenance	$6,000	$0.10
Overhead	$84,012	$1.40
Property Taxes and Insurance	$1,000	$0.02
Equipment Allocations	$10,000	$0.17
Subtotal Fixed Costs	$213,028	$3.55
SUBTOTAL VARIABLE AND FIXED COSTS	$783,449	$13.06
GENERAL AND ADMINISTRATIVE COSTS		
Selling Expense	$39,172	$0.65
Administration	$39,172	$0.65
Distribution	$39,172	$0.65
TOTAL COSTS	$900,966	$15.02

FIGURE 10A-3.

Cost estimate for Master Associates computer board, monitor, and printer

---

> PROJECTED TOTAL COSTS, of

> **Master Associates**

COS, © 1989, Dale Brethauer

BASIC PREMISES:

Number of Operators:	6
Hourly Wage Rate:	$12.10
Material Price:	$19.00
Process Yield:	95%
Sales Volume:	60,000
Total Investment:	$100,000

	$/YEAR	$/PIECE
VARIABLE COST		
Materials	$1,200,000	$20.00
Utilities	$2,000	$0.00
Subtotal Variable Costs	$1,202,000	$20.03
FIXED COSTS		
Labor	$348,429	$5.01
Equipment Maintenance	$6,000	$0.10
Overhead	$261,322	$4.36
Property Taxes and Insurance	$1,000	$0.02
Equipment Allocations	$10,000	$0.17
Subtotal Fixed Costs	$626,751	$10.45
SUBTOTAL VARIABLE AND FIXED COSTS	$1,828,751	$30.48
GENERAL AND ADMINISTRATIVE COSTS		
Selling Expense	$91,438	$1.52
Administration	$91,438	$1.52
Distribution	$91,438	$1.52
TOTAL COSTS	$2,103,064	$35.05

Competitor Cost Sheets

FIGURE 10A-4.
Cost estimate for Meds Company

PROJECTED TOTAL COSTS, of

Meds's Instrument

COS, © 1989, Dale Brethauer

BASIC PREMISES:

Number of Operators:	26
Hourly Wage Rate:	$15.00
Material Price:	$55.00
Process Yield:	95%
Sales Volume:	60,000
Total Investment:	$6,525,000

	$/YEAR	$/PIECE
VARIABLE COST		
Materials	$3,473,684	$57.89
Utilities	$130,500	$2.18
Subtotal Variable Costs	$3,604,184	$60.07
FIXED COSTS		
Labor	$1,871,728	$31.20
Equipment Maintenance	$391,500	$6.53
Overhead	$1,403,796	$23.40
Property Taxes and Insurance	$65,250	$1.09
Equipment Allocations	$652,500	$10.88
Subtotal Fixed Costs	$4,384,774	$73.08
SUBTOTAL VARIABLE AND FIXED COSTS	$7,988,958	$133.15
GENERAL AND ADMINISTRATIVE COSTS		
Selling Expense	$399,448	$6.66
Administration	$399,448	$6.66
Distribution	$399,438	$6.66
TOTAL COSTS	$9,187,302	$153.12

FIGURE 10A-5.
Cost estimate for Chockton Inc.

PROJECTED TOTAL COSTS, of

Chockton's Instrument

COS, © 1989, Dale Brethauer

BASIC PREMISES:

Number of Operators:	51
Hourly Wage Rate:	$15.00
Material Price:	$19.00
Process Yield:	95%
Sales Volume:	25,000
Total Investment:	$3,875,000

	$/YEAR	$/PIECE
VARIABLE COST		
Materials	$1,710,526	$68.42
Utilities	$77,500	$3.10
Subtotal Variable Costs	$1,788,026	$71.52
FIXED COSTS		
Labor	$3,671,466	$146.86
Equipment Maintenance	$232,500	$9.30
Overhead	$2,753,600	$110.14
Property Taxes and Insurance	$38,750	$1.55
Equipment Allocations	$387,500	$15.50
Subtotal Fixed Costs	$7,083,816	$283.35
SUBTOTAL VARIABLE AND FIXED COSTS	$8,871,843	$354.87
GENERAL AND ADMINISTRATIVE COSTS		
Selling Expense	$443,592	$17.74
Administration	$443,592	$17.74
Distribution	$443,592	$17.74
TOTAL COSTS	$10,202,619	$408.10

FIGURE 10A-6.
Projected revenues and cost savings for AMEX (thousands of dollars)

Year	Volume (thousand)	Price ($/unit)	Revenue	Incremental Revenue	Cost Savings ($/unit)	Total Cost Savings
1	55	175	9,625	−375	35	1,925
2	58	175	10,106	106	35	2,021
3	61	175	10,612	612	35	2,122
4	64	175	11,142	1,142	35	2,228
5	67	175	11,699	1,699	35	2,340
6	70	175	12,284	2,284	35	2,457
7	74	175	12,898	2,898	35	2,580
8	77	175	13,543	3,543	35	2,709
9	81	175	14,221	4,221	35	2,844
10	85	175	14,932	4,932	35	2,986

Note: Revenue was $13,000. Anything above it can be attributed to the price reduction to $175 per unit.

FIGURE 10A-7.

Ten-year cash flow after strategic costing programs for AMEX (thousands of dollars)

	Year									
	1	2	3	4	5	6	7	8	9	10
Revenue (incremental)	(375)	106	612	1,142	1,699	2,284	2,898	3,543	4,221	4,932
Other income										
Total revenue	(375)	106	612	1,142	1,699	2,284	2,898	3,543	4,221	4,932
– Cash expenses [a]	(1,925)	(2,021)	(2,122)	(2,228)	(2,340)	(2,457)	(2,580)	(2,709)	(2,844)	(2,986)
– Depreciation	380	640	380	240	240	100	0	0	0	0
Taxable income	1,170	1,487	2,354	3,130	3,799	4,641	5,478	6,252	7,065	7,918
Income taxes (40%)	468	595	942	1,252	1,520	1,856	2,191	2,501	2,826	3,167
Net income	702	892	1,412	1,878	2,279	2,785	3,287	3,751	4,239	4,751
+ Depreciation	380	640	380	240	240	100	0	0	0	0
– Investments	2,000									
Cash flow	918	1,532	1,792	2,118	2,519	2,885	3,287	3,751	4,239	4,751
Discount factor (12%)	0.893	0.797	0.712	0.636	0.567	0.507	0.452	0.404	0.36	0.322
Discounted cash flow	(820)	1,221	1,276	1,347	1,428	1,462	1,486	1,515	1,526	1,530
Cumulative discounted cash flow	(820)	401	1,678	3,025	4,453	5,916	7,401	8,917	10,443	11,973

[a] A negative cash expense is a cost savings or an increase in revenue.

CHAPTER

11

LET'S REITERATE!

The puzzle is complete! We've finished putting the pieces together, and it was a lengthy and complex assignment. You now have the tools to help maintain the financial health of your company.

You may be employed by an international multibillion-dollar corporate giant, or you may operate the corner drugstore. In terms of strategic costing, both require the same diligence in knowing what the numbers say about the business. The size of your company and your reason for doing the analysis will determine how complex your work will be.

Consider the Hawaiian Shaved Ice scenario. In my neighborhood several years ago, a man put up a neat little booth-type building in the corner of a hardware store parking lot. He painted it an eye-catching color and put a big sign on top of the building that said "Hawaiian Shaved Ice," and he was ready for business. It didn't matter that no one had ever heard of shaved ice—which by the way is very similar to the ever-popular snow cones. His stand was very appealing and he had all the available flavors listed on the front of the booth. It was only a few days until children were lined up waiting to get their paper cones filled with delicious, syrup-flavored shaved ice.

What was even more interesting was to see how many other stands of similar shapes and colors popped up in nearby neighborhoods. Some had outside seating, each had an exotic name, some were too expensive, some didn't put as much syrup, some sold other items like boiled peanuts and hot dogs, and some were hard to get to because of poor street accessibility or lack of parking. Some were located in highly populated areas and some in the suburbs.

Some of the stands only lasted one season, some held on for a couple of years, but only a few are still open for business today. What made the difference? Each had the same opportunity—yet some couldn't make a go of the business.

All these little businesses had to figure their costs, how to price themselves to be competitive yet make a profit, how to come up with new ways to market, how to maintain business after the "new" wore off.

The rules are the same for every business in the marketplace today. The companies that continue to thrive will be those that strategically place themselves in the forefront, lower their costs, know what's going on with the competition, and make wise decisions concerning expansion or even downsizing. Whether you make a product or provide a service, if you use the skills taught in this book, you don't have to wish and hope; you can put numbers in their proper places in the equations provided and see exactly what your picture looks like!

Frequently Asked Questions

I list here some of the questions people ask at strategic costing seminars. I hope that your questions, too, are answered here; if not, my address is at the end of the chapter, and I invite you to send me any question you have about strategic costing.

1. *Will this process work in a small business?*
   Yes, the Strategic Costing Process has been taught to and is used by large, medium-size, and small companies.

2. *Most of my supplier production runs are small lots. How do I estimate labor if an operator only works on a product a small percentage of the year?*

If labor is calculated for less than a full year, you need to modify the labor equation. Recall the original equation:

No. of operators × Wage rate ×4,800

The constant 4,800 in this equation is obtained by multiplying 52 weeks times 40 hours per week (2,080). That number is then multiplied by all the following factors:

Vacation 1.11
Relief 1.23
Benefits 1.3
Supervision 1.3

(You'll find the factors in Chapter 3.) To adjust the equation, take the number of hours worked in a full year, 2,080, and (1) replace it with actual hours worked or (2) multiply it by percentage of a full year worked, depending on which you know. Also, if the product is produced in less than a full year, you might want to ignore the relief and vacation factors. The final equation is then:

No. of operators × Wage rate × Hours × (1.3*1.3)

3. *I have talked with our finance department, and they say our company overheads are 100 percent of labor. You said to use 75 percent of labor for overheads. What should I do?*
   Use 100 percent of labor for overheads for your company, your supplier, and your competitor. My estimating numbers are excellent. However, adjusting the equations to factors specific to your industry will make your version of the cost-estimating model even more accurate. That is why I do not lock the cells holding the estimating equations on the spreadsheet. Please modify them according to your own information.

4. *In my industry, utilities are usually a major portion of costs. What should I do?*
   Utilities are driven by equipment investment. Talk with your finance department to get a percentage of investment to use

for annual utilities. A good generic default is 2 percent. Although I have studied some industries that go as high as 10 percent, these are few. If your industry is one of them, please modify the percentage. It will make the cost-estimating model more accurate.

5. *Won't suppliers be skeptical if you ask too many questions while you're touring their facilities?*
   Yes, that is why it's important to meet with your team before the actual tour. Make sure the questions are not too obvious, and don't bombard your tour guide with too many pointed questions.

6. *How much time does it take to perform the Strategic Costing Process?*
   I can't answer this question directly because the time varies, depending on several factors: the product or service being analyzed, your supplier, your competitor(s), the internal team you put together, support from management, and resources of both people and money available to run the process. The resource requirements may be substantial, so strategic costing should be used for only your "big ticket" products. Also, hiring a consultant to help to implement this process can really improve the efficiency of the study and its chances for success.

7. *What products or services cannot use the Strategic Costing Process, and in particular, the cost-estimating model?*
   After ten years plus of applying the Strategic Costing Process, I have run across very few products and services that did not benefit from this process. The cost-estimating model, in particular, is extremely accurate for most products and services. If the model is adapted slightly to the specific industry, it is even more accurate.

8. *After I identify programs to achieve a target cost, how do I know how large the NPV must be to be considered good?*
   Any project with a positive NPV is worth pursuing. A positive NPV means the investment will earn the cost of capital every year for a ten-year period, plus an additional amount.

9. *Why do you run a cash flow analysis for ten years?*
   Cash flow may be calculated for the life of the project if that is to be less than ten years. However, when comparing projects, the same analysis time period needs to be used. A ten-year analysis allows depreciation to run out and project equilibrium to be reached.

10. *Freight is a major cost for my industry. How should I adjust the cost-estimating model?*
    Freight that is interplant transportation to a warehouse is part of general and administrative costs. Beyond that, freight is usually paid by the customer. If not, you must include it as an add-on to the cost-estimating model.

If you have other questions or comments, please write to me at the following address:

Brethauer Consulting Group, Inc.
Dale M. Brethauer, President
755 Beversrede Trail, Suite 1201
West Chester, PA 19382
610/388-3260

or e-mail me at:

dale.m.brethauer@usa.dupont.com

INDEX